Creating Bodies

RELATIONAL PERSPECTIVES BOOK SERIES

LEWIS ARON AND ADRIENNE HARRIS
Series Editors

Volume 1
Rita Wiley McCleary
Conversing with Uncertainty: Practicing Psychotherapy in a Hospital Setting

Volume 2
Charles Spezzano
Affect in Psychoanalysis: A Clinical Synthesis

Volume 3
Neil Altman
The Analyst in the Inner City: Race, Class, and Culture Through a Psychoanalytic Lens

Volume 4
Lewis Aron
A Meeting of Minds: Mutuality in Psychoanalysis

Volume 5
Joyce A. Slochower
Holding and Psychoanalysis: A Relational Perspective

Volume 6
Barbara Gerson, ed.
The Therapist as a Person: Life Crises, Life Choices, Life Experiences, and Their Effects on Treatment

Volume 7
Charles Spezzano and Gerald J. Gargiulo, editors
Soul on the Couch: Spirituality, Religion, and Morality in Contemporary Psychoanalysis

Volume 8
Donnel B. Stern
Unformulated Experience: From Dissociation to Imagination in Psychoanalysis

Volume 9
Stephen A. Mitchell
Influence and Autonomy in Psychoanalysis

Volume 10
Neil J. Skolnick and David E. Scharff, editors
Fairbairn, Then and Now

Volume 11
Stuart A. Pizer
Building Bridges: Negotiation of Paradox in Psychoanalysis

Volume 12
Lewis Aron and Frances Sommer Anderson, editors
Relational Perspectives on the Body

Volume 13
Karen Maroda
Seduction, Surrender, and Transformation: Emotional Engagement in the Analytic Process

Volume 14
Stephen A. Mitchell and Lewis Aron, editors
Relational Psychoanalysis: The Emergence of a Tradition

Volume 15
Rochelle G. K. Kainer
The Collapse of the Self and Its Therapeutic Restoration

Volume 16
Kenneth A. Frank
Psychoanalytic Participation: Action, Interaction, and Integration

Volume 17
Sue Grand
The Reproduction of Evil: A Clinical and Cultural Perspective

Volume 18
Steven Cooper
Objects of Hope: Exploring Possibility and Limit in Psychoanalysis

Volume 19
James S. Grotstein
Who Is the Dreamer Who Dreams the Dream? A Study of Psychic Presences

Volume 20
Stephen A. Mitchell
Relationality: From Attachment to Intersubjectivity

Volume 21
Peter Carnochan
Looking for Ground: Countertransference, and the Problem of Value in Psychoanalysis

Volume 22
Muriel Dimen
Sexuality, Intimacy, Power

Volume 23
Susan W. Coates, Jane L. Rosenthal and Daniel S. Schechter, editors
September 11: Trauma and Human Bonds

Volume 24
Randall Lehmann Sorenson
Minding Spirituality

Volume 25
Adrienne Harris
Gender as Soft Assembly

Volume 26
Emanuel Berman
Impossible Training: A Relational View of Psychoanalytic Education

Volume 27
Carlo Strenger
The Designed Self: Psychoanalysis and Contemporary Identities

Volume 28
Lewis Aron and Adrienne Harris, editors
Relational Psychoanalysis, Vol. 2: Innovation and Expansion

Volume 29
Sebastiano Santostefano
Child Therapy in the Great Outdoors: A Relational View

Volume 30
James T. McLaughlin
The Healer's Bent: Solitude and Dialogue in the Clinical Encounter

Volume 31
Danielle Knafo and Kenneth Feiner
Unconscious Fantasies and the Relational World

Volume 32
Sheldon Bach
Getting from Here to There: Analytic Love, Analytic Process

Volume 33
Katie Gentile
Creating Bodies: Eating Disorders as Self-Destructive Survival

Creating Bodies

Eating Disorders as Self-Destructive Survival

KATIE GENTILE

THE ANALYTIC PRESS

2007 Mahwah, New Jersey London

Published by
The Analytic Press, Inc., Publishers
Editorial Offices:
10 Industrial Avenue
Mahwah, NJ 07430

www.analyticpress.com

Cover design by Kathryn Houghtaling Lacey.

Library of Congress Cataloging-in-Publication Data

ISBN: 0-88163-438-7

Gentile, Katie.
Creating bodies : eating disorders as self-destructive survival / Katie Gentile.
p. cm.

Printed in the United States of America

10 9 8 7 6 5 4 3 2 1

To Hannah and Meg,

for maintaining a loving friendship across

continents, seas, and decades

Contents

Acknowledgments

So many people were involved directly and indirectly in the writing of this book. I have to thank my professors/friends Mary Sue Richardson and Berenice Fisher, who introduced me to the wonderful world of feminist methods of inquiry. Without their unfailing faith and support, this diary analysis would not have been possible.

While writing, I spent each Wednesday for four years with my classmates and teachers at the Institute for Contemporary Psychotherapy (ICP), where I became more and more enthralled with psychoanalytic theory. In particular, I owe intellectual and clinical debts to my mentors: the late Adria Schwartz, Ed Corrigan, Stephen Knoblauch, Tony Bass, and my group supervisor, Jody Messler Davies. I must also acknowledge the analytic work of Holly Levenkron and Amy Schaffer, who, in their respective ways, enabled me to write. While this book is about Hannah, my patients at ICP and the students I work with at John Jay College have also shaped this analysis by continually reminding me of the impact of trauma on time and on our capacities to live in the world and of the many, many creative ways of resisting.

I had the good fortune to have astute and expansive editorial assistance on parts of this analysis from Margaret Black, Donnel Stern, and Lawrence Jacobson. They each asked unique and thoughtful questions.

It is impossible to find words to express my appreciation to Lew Aron, Adrienne Harris, and The Analytic Press. They all maintain such high standards of innovative psychoanalytic writing that to work with them was a dream. Adrienne's editorial feedback and general enthusiasm was invigorating and made the process an intellectual treat.

More personally, I want to thank my friends and colleagues Meena Alhuwalia, Emmelien Brouwers, Jennifer Capobianco, Dan

Cuddy, Jane Gilman, and Gigi Keenan for asking the right questions and providing excellent feedback during conversations. In particular, I want to acknowledge Helen Hurwitz and Tamar Rothenberg for their solidifying comments on the proposal and specific chapters. Thanks also to the musicians I play with who help keep the "creative use of language" alive.

I must thank my family, in particular my parents, who instilled in me a passion for thinking, reading, and analyzing—and my cats, who remind me each day that meaning emanates from the body. Lastly, I thank Rob Weisberg, my musical consultant and partner, for creating the soundtrack to write to.

Chapter 1

Introducing the Main Characters

You are just a thought that someone
Somewhere somehow feels you should be here
And it's so for real to touch
To smell, to feel, to know where you are here.

—Arthur Lee, *A House Is Not a Motel*

Imagine walking through the world with no knowledge of who you are, what you look like, where you end or begin. Nothing is "for real." Your only movement is in response to others, what they want for you, from you. You cease to exist when not embodied by other people's desires. This is life in Hannah's diaries.

This book is an analysis of Hannah's[1] diaries. Hannah wrote 16 diaries in 18 years, spanning the time from when she was 14 until she was 32 years old. These books tell many different stories about her life. There is the story of her backstabbing adolescent friends. There are stories of her emotionally and sexually abusive

[1] Hannah is a pseudonym chosen by the participant. All her identifying characteristics and those of the people she writes about have been changed.

parents; her father's bulimia; her mother's habit of not letting Hannah bathe without also sharing the tub with her; how together her parents administered medicines by pinning Hannah down on a table, prying her mouth open, and holding it shut until she swallowed. There are the stories of men: one after the other, who easily guide a dissociated Hannah into alleys, locked offices, and hospital rooms for unnamed sexual activities. There is the story of her 18-year relationship with bulimia—the vomiting, the lists of foods, the calorie counts, the obsession with ordering her closet, scrutinizing her body in the mirror, the ritualized masturbation, the laxatives and diuretics, the constant comparisons with other women, all orgasmically culminating in the moment of absolute calm and clean after a purge. Then there is the overarching story of her marriage to an abusive, controlling man who made no room for her. Last, there is a rare story of transformation and healing. This change came at a price, however, and it does not follow a neat narrative structure.

As in a psychoanalytic session, Hannah's story is told not only through the content of her words (her voice) but also through the structure of her text (her body, unconscious). And, as in a session, her story is given life only as the reader/analyst allows it to work on his or her body and mind. As the reader, this process was not pleasant. While the strangled rhythm of the content often lulled me to sleep (into submission), the structure and process of her text became assaultive. In Hannah's diaries, dramatic stories are told with little affect by a seemingly invisible author who has no response to anything. She collects events by throwing them onto the page without meaning-making. The binding of her diary book becomes the only skin holding her together. As she rattles off her life as though it were a grocery list, she creates a narrative that can seem like first, second, and third person simultaneously. It was often impossible to distinguish who was doing what to whom.

For me as a reader, that was terrifying. If absences communicate the unconscious within the relational space (Ogden, 1994), then I spent three years with Hannah's unconscious sadistically toying with me. I became enveloped within her murky world of unspoken invasion, seamless merging, manipulation, submission, and control. I found myself not only a passive (or active) "witness" to abuse, but a partner in it, subject to it, watching her be violated, being violated in turn, and, in writing this, becoming the violator, exposing both Hannah and her text. Given that analyses are also exercises in narrativizing the analyst (Harris, 1998), I had to allow myself to be transformed in order to relate to the diaries. Thus, different aspects of my self had to come into being in relation to Hannah's text, including my envy, competition, righteousness, empathy, and respect, as well as my own past, which eerily mirrored hers.

This relational muddle became clear and fruitful only when our experiences were able to be "embraced by time" (Loewald, 1980). Time is not an object to be found or a narrative chronology, but, rather, is the capacity to make meaning of experience by linking cause and effect, differentiating past, present, and future. Time creates the space where the "unspeakable" can become symbolized. It emerges only through relational interaction, from the transitional or liminal space where the culturally constructed distinctions of mind-body, self-other, intrapsychic-culture are negotiated. Thus, by virtue of its function as a transitional phenomenon, time can bring the culture into psychoanalytic development and agentic subjectivity into feminist theory. This integration has particular importance for an analysis of eating disorders and sexual abuse.

The body is the first site of relational control, and the mouth in particular is the first orifice of expression, taking in, spitting up and out, and speaking desire. It is also central to what the culture values: that which is speakable and symbolizable. Eating disorders enact this struggle, but, by taking the adult or adolescent body as the site of control, these disorders use a culturally marked body patrolled by categories of gender, race, class, ethnicity, sexual orientation, and religion. The struggle is not merely about parental dynamics; it is constituted by the refracting control and corresponding resistance that occurs as one walks, talks, interacts, and continually comes into being within a particular social world.

As the identified bodies of the culture, women with eating disorders are expressing something quite important for both the individual and the culture. Thus, an in-depth analysis of eating disorders that explores the intrapsychic, relational, and cultural dynamics is an important entrée to examining the complicated relationship between resistance and traumatic repetitions occurring not only in eating disorders but in everyday life. These simultaneous expressions help locate the space of interaction between the social and the intrapsychic unconscious. Working clinically from these spaces creates the potential for individual and cultural transformation.

Analyzing Hannah's diaries was a relational endeavor similar to a clinical case study, but there are limits to this label. I was never in the position of her therapist. As her self-destruction escalated, I could watch her attempts to overdose without having to intervene. I had the luxury of time and space, as it were, to analyze her diaries. Focusing on the diaries, however, provided little opportunity to ask clarifying questions. Instead, I approached her diaries as an externalized representation of her evolving capacities to symbolize her experience. This representation was captured and displayed in her text, providing a unique longitudinal view of her transformation. So, this relational analysis is in some ways more constrained and limited than that of a clinical session, while in other ways it is much more free.

Timing Our Relationship

I met Hannah through a mutual friend who was my colleague in graduate school. She and Hannah had grown up together outside London. We were brought together because Hannah was seeking someone to analyze and help her publish her years of diaries, and I was looking for someone who would collaborate in an in-depth study of bulimia. After some introductory mail correspondence (Hannah still lives in London), Hannah visited New York and brought her diaries. Given the brief introduction to Hannah so far, it may not be surprising that she entrusted me with all her diaries after only one meeting.

Although I had initially conceptualized us as working on the analysis together, owing to the distance between us, we decided that I would write the analysis of her diaries and then fly to London to meet with her so she could read it and respond verbally or within the text, as she chose. This way I would be present and able to assess if the process had a negative impact on her. (See Gentile, 2000, for further exploration of this process.)

I worked on the analysis for three years with the "real" Hannah being only an ever-present shadow of a future reader. She sent the occasional postcard; we spoke on the phone a few times a year, but discussion was limited to her giving me updates about her changing life and my providing her with a sketchy timeline. Once a solid draft of the analysis was written, we met in London for 10 hours of audiotaped meetings, during which time we discussed her responses to reading the analysis, reread her diaries, and talked about her experiences of the process in general. She decided to write her initial responses to reading the analysis within the text, using words and symbols she created to convey and represent her experience. She did not want to write her entire response, however; she wanted to be able to explain them to me verbally in person.

It is important to note that at this point in her life Hannah was not in therapy. I suggested that she return for at least the duration of this research, and she agreed. She entered into a weekly group. Because I am focusing on her diaries, the impact of this therapy is beyond the scope of this book.[2]

---

[2] Hannah was in and out of therapy with two different individual therapists for the first two years of her adult diaries, and with a single couple's therapist for the first year. It is unclear how much effect these therapists had on her life or on the diaries. For instance, although she often notes when she sees her therapists, she does not mention when she changed therapists. I knew only because she suddenly wrote a different name. I do not know why she had a new therapist or how she felt about the change. She meticulously tracked her weight, her food intake, her sexual experiences, but little of her interpersonal relationships. Certainly, these therapies and other interpersonal relationships occurred in tandem with her diaries, but, from the analysis and my own experiences with Hannah, I am not sure how much of another person she could let in. Because the impact of her therapy is not conveyed in her diaries, it is beyond the scope of this book.

The Fruitful Silver Lining of a Partially Disembodied Analysis

I've put a pebble in my shoe
Every step I am with you
I just stumble along
To the beat of a child's drum
My heart is on the line
Can all my wonders be true.

—Eugene Kelly, "Pebble/Shoe"

Interestingly, not having contact with Hannah while writing the analysis created a surprisingly fruitful space between us. In the absence of relating directly, we both created characters named Hannah and Katie with whom to relate during the analysis. For her, Hannah was not only her study name, it became an objectified version of herself. As she described, knowing that I was attending closely to the self-destructive and troubled Hannah captured in the diaries enabled her to create the space necessary to observe her life and to transform it. Indeed, during the research process she was able to end an emotionally abusive relationship and begin to see men who were kinder to her. She also described becoming more at peace with herself and able to take long holidays from her work life, which had previously consumed her. She described doing this "alone in the presence of another" (Winnicott, 1958b) character, a mythical therapist/researcher/friend named Katie who was spending "gobs of time" and energy on her life, analyzing her, preparing to tell her all about herself.

The Hannah I created was a confidante, someone with whom I was seamlessly merged in a transcendent understanding of each other's experience, which was a double-edged sword. I "knew" her and by this knowing was implicitly recognized as an omnipotent rescuer, healer, friend. But I also felt enveloped by her chaos, pried open, invaded, and used. Walking around in Hannah's texts was a requirement for the analysis, but it made me feel crazy, violated, rigidly controlled, and bulimic. No place was safe. Whether I was walking down the street, talking to friends, sleeping, or eating, snippets of her undigested abuse kept popping up out of the blue. I would hear her words come out of my mouth, her thoughts began shaping mine, her weight influenced mine, her dieting coaxed mine. As she began entering my own analytic space, I felt penetrated like chattel, being used to process experiences that were not even mine. But Hannah's history of abuse became a transformational wrench for me within this analysis.

I cannot remember a time in my life when food and body image did not define me. Throughout elementary school, disordered eating and the other panoply of symptoms that color eating problems were the frame through which I understood and engaged with the world. There was a bright side to that, though, for they had amazing magical powers of explanation. They could be called on to provide a perfect, deadening order to interpersonal interactions and thus made life safe and possible. They functioned like a fundamentalist religious ideology, becoming my dogma for living. According to Winnicott (1960), religion (dogma) is created when one cannot have faith in ongoingness in the face of uncertainty and the unknown. Without such faith there can be no capacity to believe in worth and meaningfulness. Eating disorders can provide such a cohering dogma, and, because they are supported by the culture in so many ways, they can seem a perfect solution in the face of terror, chaos, and potential fragmentation.

So, when I was sexually abused at the age of 10, the uncertainty and terror of the situation was completely subsumed by shame and humiliation, not of my having been victimized, but of my body and weight. In my mind (and body) my experiences of abuse were collapsed and integrated into my humiliation of being identified as fat. In my mind, I was abused because I ate too much. If I could just conquer my eating problems (read: desires, appetites, body), I would be impenetrable. Being abused became an issue of my will, not my victimization. I took control of terrifying incidents such that they literally ceased to exist in my mind. With this foundation, it was unavoidable that my eating behaviors would morph into full-blown bulimia by the time I was 15.

When I began reading Hannah's diaries, I knew little about her life. I knew she had had bulimia and I knew her ex-husband had been somewhat abusive, but that was all. Entering her world chronologically through her text, I spent the first months reading her adolescence. So when I began reading her adult diaries, I already had constructed a particular image of Hannah from my relationship to her adolescent text. This image did not include any abuse because, until this point, she had not written a word of her abusive experiences. But about a third of the way into her adult diaries, she began making vague allusions to what seemed to be sexually abusive encounters in her childhood with her parents and a priest. I was stunned and somehow felt responsible. How did I not know this? When had these incidents occurred? Where was I when she was being abused and why hadn't I told anyone? This countertransferential response of hyperresponsibility soon shifted into denial.

Many of my female friends described experiences similar to mine and Hannah's while they were growing up. In a way, part of me was trained to believe such encounters were a normal, unfortunate, but unavoidable introduction into female sexuality (see Haaken, 1998). The high frequency made it difficult to label it as "abuse." Since then I have seen a number of patients, students, and friends who were abused and labeled it as such. But, somehow, abuse was a label saved to help others, not me and not Hannah in relation to me. Then I had a meeting with my advisor, who, after reading an excerpt from Hannah's diaries, exclaimed with deep empathy (not judgment) about the trauma Hannah must have experienced after being sexually abused. Trauma? So abuse was not normal, after all. She/I wasn't to blame. She/I did not have to be humiliated in narrating this part of the story. I realized that I had to reconceptualize both myself and Hannah simultaneously. My own historical narrative collapsed, and, like Hannah, I used my text as a space within which to do the necessary re-creating.

Texts are fascinating spaces. They can become "usable" in the Winnicottian sense because they provide the freedom to improvise holding and hiding, contact and differentiation, in other words, temporality—space and time. Both Hannah's and my texts provided a space within which to create transitional bodies that were neither inner nor outer, self nor other, mind nor body. They served as a transitional space between mind–object existence (Corrigan and Gordon, 1995) and psyche–soma integration, between having an abundance of undifferentiated dangerous time and being able to yield to and be "embraced by time" (Loewald, 1980). As Searles (1979) observed, the patient heals a part of the analyst in the process of being healed. I learned about my own temporal linking by watching Hannah's. As I watched her create time, I learned to create it myself by theorizing it in the analysis. She literally pulled me along.

The theory of time presented in this book served as my anchor (Bromberg, 1998) throughout this complicated endeavor. It is a theory formulated to explore resistance and complicity, trauma and resilience as they emerge within culturally created, relational contexts. This theory of temporal linking is described in the following chapter.

Even the Best Laid Plans

The nature of relational collaboration is cocreation, which demands a certain degree of flexibility. Another of my original plans that had to shift was inviting Hannah to speak for herself by having her write her responses in the text of my analysis. This was supposed to represent in print our relational dynamics from the analysis. But my struggle to live with/in her diaries altered this intention.

First, I realized that asking her to write her responses was a huge, gut-wrenching, exhilarating, terrifying task, one that seemed especially sadistic once I realized that Hannah had great difficulties symbolizing her experiences in her diaries. Second, even if she could easily write her experiences, the fact was that the trauma in her diaries easily seeped into my skin not only because of my own past, but because it was not symbolized in words; it was held in unconscious spaces of the text where it easily catches the reader unawares. I could not be certain that having this trauma locked in time within my text would render it less potent to Hannah as she read my analysis.

Furthermore, communicating through a text would confine our relationship to a one-dimensional arena, the same arena that Hannah was good at writing herself out of in the diaries. In her text, she was not a subject of her own experience and desires. Planning a textual interaction may have reenacted this objectification and foreclosed her participation as an experiencing subject within our relationship.

Last, after reading incident after incident of others' taking Hannah over for their needs and her engaging in relationships with no concern for herself, how could the dynamics of power and invasion that swirled around her not shape our collaboration? I did not want to be any more of an invader than I already had been, and I did not wish to be invaded any more than I felt I had. As Stacey (1988) cautioned, collaboration does not address issues of power, authority, or representation; and, through the creation of this closer relationship, it can provide new and perhaps more destructive opportunities for exploitation. Thus, a form of caring entered into the situation.

Caring is an interesting maneuver in relationships (Tronto, 1996; Fisher, 2001). During our collaboration, Hannah sometimes identified my "caring" as a way of controlling our relationship and the analysis. For instance, during our meetings I often felt that our dialogue was founded on the mutual activity of tunneling inside Hannah. Yet, when I asked for her take on the situation, what I experienced as invading she seemed to identify as being recognized. I explored this reaction in light of her potential desires to please me or her history of being constituted within invasive and exposing relationships, and she repeatedly responded that the process felt "fine." I walked the fine line between protecting her from invasion and respecting the collaboration and her desires to shape her own representation. She felt not only that my caring was not necessary here, but that, functioning to protect myself in relation to her, it threatened to become an impediment to the collaboration.

Certainly, caring was based on my authority as a clinician who supposedly "knows" about trauma survivors and women with bulimia and what I was learning about Hannah from the diaries. But exploring her choices here implied assumptions on my part that I knew Hannah better than she was able consciously to know herself, which was not a particularly empowering relational stance from which to engage her. It was almost impossible to know when my caring was protecting Hannah and when it was saving me from having to connect to her.

Collaborating also required a significant shift in the process of writing. Instead of the already complicated process of writing what I "knew," it became a process of my writing as if I were Hannah reading the analysis. On one hand, I felt that her future reading authorized me to write freely, knowing she could "talk back" against what I said. On the other, more powerful hand, to help create the space for a transformative relationship through which Hannah would be able to talk back, I felt I had to take great care of her with each thought I conveyed. As in a session, I had to think about the function of each point I was making. Was it important to her or to me? Would it help her? Was I using too much psychological jargon? The function of the research had to expand to include not only impressing a committee and being awarded a doctorate, but also writing for Hannah's comprehension.

For instance, in the analysis I tried to eschew psychological labels for fear of hurting, objectifying or, pathologizing Hannah. This avoidance was important not only for a textured analysis but also to maintain and represent some of the many complicated positions Hannah takes in relationships. Hannah's subjectivity is there and not there, embodied and disembodied, victim and abuser simultaneously. Writing of her only as a victim or an abuser in S–M relationships pinned her down like a sacrificed butterfly; it was too easy. From a label there could be no movement, no intricacy, and no hope for Hannah to get out. Of course, I did not want her to read such a painfully foreclosing analysis of her diaries.

I did, however, use sadomasochistic as well as other labels. Hannah wanted them; dare I say, she needed them. Having read her diaries, I saw clearly that Hannah seemed to wear psychiatric labels proudly, not only as a psychic skin holding her together, defining in–out, self–other, but also as a way to display herself publicly. My aversion to labels was a denial of my antipathy to that side of Hannah, and she caught it. So writing to be read and then collaborating created many levels of tension to navigate and altered my text.

Writing to "Know"

In this book, I claim to "know" something of Hannah, and in this "knowing" I take her over, claiming to "know" what happened in the diaries, to "know" what was best for her at times. I not only invaded her experience as represented in her diaries, but I colonized her by translating it into my theories within my text for the advancement of my Ph.D. and now, with this book, for tenure as a professor. I literally became an authority on the basis of my knowing Hannah.

But knowing also created the space necessary for dialogue. Only by creating a position from which I could speak knowledgeably could Hannah "see" where I was coming from in the analysis so she could counter it, agree with it, or just ask questions, which she did. As Sampson (1996) notes, transformative relationships must be embodied. To embody our relationship, I had to enter into the analysis to collaborate with a distinct body, a distinct position of knowing. The "anchoring of subjectivity in *its* body is the condition of coherent identity, and, moreover, the condition under which the subject *has a perspective* on the world" (Grosz, 1995, p. 89). I did not have this distinctly bound, visible body when I was drowning in her text or caring for her by protecting her from what I "knew." My relational body was created by my temporally organizing, symbolizing, and integrating my history with my experiences of her diaries through the authority of theory and knowing. Only with a distinct body could I collaborate with, not merge and invade, the real-life Hannah. Only then could I represent a position from which we could begin to engage, negotiate, and relate. I had to attempt to know fluidly, to let ideas flow in and out, without completely losing my bearings.

About This Text

As I have mentioned, during our collaboration, Hannah decided to read the analysis and respond with symbols and sometimes a few words written in pencil in the spaces between paragraphs. In our last meeting, she asked me to read the comments and symbols aloud to her and she elaborated orally with her responses, thoughts, and associations. Thus, her interaction with the analysis was layered. There were the initial, abbreviated responses and the elaborate comments, the latter of which could not occur when she was relating with the text alone but needed an embodied relational context.[1]

Many chapters and sections of chapters begin with long quotes from Hannah's diaries. These quotes and other longer examples from Hannah's diaries are differentiated from my analysis typographically.

The Subject of This Analysis

Hannah wrote 16 diaries in all, ranging from the shortest—24 doubled-spaced, typed pages (one of the adult diaries)—to the longest—175 typed pages. The majority are 75–80 pages. I typed her diaries to enable me to read and compare them. I structured the text to mirror hers and noted changes in handwriting and spacing where appropriate. I divided them into two sections.

The Ease of Adolescence

The adolescent section comprises three diaries covering the years 1977, 1978, and 1979, when Hannah was 14–17. These diaries are of a quality completely different from those she wrote as an adult;

---

[1] These interactions are represented within this book in different ways. Hannah's comments and symbols are written in brackets in italics in the sections she reponded to *[Hannah: Hannah's comments]*. Sometimes she noted she resonated with certain paragraphs or sections in particular. These have been set off from the rest of the book by a different font. I use footnotes at the bottom of the page to explain Hannah's comments.

the adolescent had a thread to follow, a structure with which to interact. They are written in date books that have a proscribed space for each date, so the very structure of the books has a temporality. Each of these diaries is the size of a small, hardcover book, and the first two are actually office date books with a week represented on each two-page spread. As one opens the diary, each page has predetermined seven-line sections for each of the seven days of the week, and each is dated with the day, date, and year. There are actually eight, seven-line sections, one undated at the top of each right-hand page of the spread. Hannah tended to use this extra space to elaborate on one of the days of the week. It was never left empty. The 1979 diary is like an office diary, but with the day, date, and year at the top of each page, giving a full page for each day. Hannah usually used the entire page for each day. This is the longest diary.

Throughout these diaries her handwriting is completely static. She writes in ink, with small, balanced cursive letters; she does not print. Again, she takes up all the space provided by the books and seldom creates new lines to complete a thought. She never scrunches up her handwriting to fit into a line or has scratchouts; thus her thoughts seem to have been created to fit into the space.

The diaries throw the reader into a village outside London, where days are filled with such activities as school, volunteer work, piano lessens, choir, going to the theater, and babysitting. Hannah has crushes on boys; she has a regular group of friends; she fights with her mother. There is little beyond these fights that describes her home life, and there is no mention of what they fight about. I know she is an only child, she attends an all-girls public school (equivalent to private school in the United States), and her parents were older than average when she was born: her mother was 36, her father was 48.

In general, there is a certain rhythm and boundedness to these entries, and each begins with the time and way Hannah woke up, for example, "Mum woke me at . . ." or "Had breakfast in bed . . .". The entries primarily cover the social interactions at school, whether she thought it was a "good" or a "bad" day—based on the level of conflict between friends. Initially, these diaries were quite boring, entry after entry detailing daily events of other people in a strangling, perfectly measured fashion. Hannah was virtually absent, except as the invisible narrator. She quotes other people's comments, which made her seem even more invisible, for she did not even interpret conversation.

Gradually, a melodramatic and riveting narration of her school social life emerged. Story after story of friendships created only to be ripped apart through vicious fights, all behind the others' backs, is told in detail by the "peacemaker," Hannah. In-depth descriptions of the dynamics of her female friendships are fascinating and familiar, as they construct, destroy, and reconstruct passionate relationships that rival traditional narratives of heterosexual romantic love. Men and boys are on the periphery while female friendships tumultuously endure. Hannah's parents make brief appearances, but they are erased in favor of her friendships.

The rhythm changes drastically in the middle of the 1979 diary, when Hannah leaves school at the age of 16 to work in a bank and attend college. She writes about each task she does and how long it takes her. She details what she eats for lunch, how much it costs, where she eats dinner, and how much that costs. Her school friends, who had previously taken up almost all her entries, are rarely mentioned. These entries are also the only entries in the adolescent diaries that do not always take up the entire page provided for each day. By December, the entries have shortened, and Hannah even begins to skip many days in a row.

In the last months of the last adolescent diary, the narration winds tighter and tighter around an author who is slipping through the cracks. The friendships that meant life or death chillingly disappear, never to be referred to again. Hannah, who was already a tenuous presence in the diaries, is utterly lost, replaced by oppressive details of food and money. Although Hannah never wrote about it, it is obvious she was descending into anorexia and bulimia.

The diaries end here, and racing to the adult diaries provided no relief from feelings of having lost someone, because the adult diaries present a whole new cast of characters, including a new, very troubled adult Hannah. The answers to my most pressing questions (What was going on? Where did her friends go? Why did she leave school?) would emerge only gradually, in her own time, as she was able to symbolize them for herself well into her adult diaries.

The Adult Diaries

There are 13 adult diaries, written during a three-year period from 1992–1995, when Hannah was 30–33. It is in these diaries that Hannah remembers her childhood and early adulthood. At times, the diaries are written as if she was 12 or 25; it is not merely that she is retrospectively catching us up with events of her life, she is literally learning to remember them. Consequently, she often writes of events as if they have just happened, which is extremely confusing to a reader. For instance, I did not know her father had died until the fifth adult diary. Until then, I thought the stories of him were in her current time.

The diaries begin when Hannah is admitted to the hospital after her mother died of cancer. As I would learn, her father had died of cancer 10 years before. She was admitted by a psychiatrist with whom she had an outpatient consultation for bereavement issues. He felt that she was so depressed she was a threat to herself. She asked to be admitted to an eating disorders unit and was sent to one in a very nice private hospital. At this point in time she had been married for nine years to an abusive and controlling man, Eric. As is common in cases of trauma, although her home life was a repetition of her abusive childhood relationships, her public persona (Davies and Frawley, 1992, 1994) was one of competence; she was the director of the human resources department in a multinational company.

The first 10 diaries are nondescript, lined notebooks, half the size of a regular lined 8-1/2 by 11-inch page. For the first eight diaries, Hannah wrote in the notebook on one side of the page. She then turned the book over and began the second diary on the other side of the page. Hence each notebook contains two diaries. They are each numbered by Hannah—1/2, 3/4, 5/6, and 7/8. The last two notebooks, diaries, 9 and 10, are each a single diary. These are the longest of the adult diaries, as she wrote on each page, front and back, for one diary. The last three diaries are dated only by month; they are not numbered. Each page is lined, each entry dated. She has stapled in pages where she made entries on different paper and then attached them to the diary in chronological order. The last diary is a small, ring-bound notebook consisting almost entirely of lists.

Unlike the adolescent diaries, these books had no external boundary of either space or time. Spatially, an entry could be a paragraph, a page, or an entire book. A day could be any length. The time between entries could be hours, days, or minutes. The only temporality was that conveyed within her text, the externalized representation of her internal experience of temporal chaos. Indeed, many entries seemed expulsive in nature, as if she was unable to hold back her writing. Although, I must say, once I had transcribed the diaries onto the computer, much of the urgency was lost. This loss made me realize that the expulsive quality I am referring to had been cocreated by her handwriting, which made me want to read faster and faster as it looked as though it was written faster and faster. It was impossible not to become caught up in the feverishness of the story. Her handwriting changed within an entry, unlike her adolescent writing, which seemed so precise as to have been typed.

These diaries, filling in the cracks of her childhood, tell the stories of abuse that were absent in her adolescent diaries. As she links her past memories to her present, she unravels and attempts suicide three times. Through her fragmentation, however, she recreates herself, a story told in both the content and the structure of her adult text.

The Relational Space of a Text Analysis

The method of analysis I used is an integration of relational psychoanalysis with different forms of inquiry from feminist studies of women's lives in anthropology (e.g., Bateson, 1989; Young, 1991; Mahoney and Yngvesson, 1992; Behar, 1993; Visweswaran, 1994), sociology (e.g., Mumby, 1993; Richardson, 1995; Naples and Clark, 1996; Stanley, 1996), psychology and education (e.g., Henriques et al., 1984; Lather, 1988; Hollway, 1989; Walkerdine, 1990, 1994; Fine, 1994a, b, 1996; Lather and Smithies, 1997; Tolman and Brydon-Miller, 2001), studies of narrative (e.g., McAdams and Ochberg, 1988; Denzin, 1989; Polkinghorne, 1991, 1996; Riessman, 1993; Bruner, 1994; Manning and Cullum-Swan, 1994; Josselson, 1996; Widdershoven and Smits, 1996), and studies on women's autobiographical writing (e.g., de Lauretis, 1986; Heilbrun, 1988; Peterson and Stewart, 1990; West, 1992; Smith, 1993, 1995; Stanley, 1993, 1996; Warhol and Herndl, 1997; Smith and Watson, 1998; Young-Bruehl, 1998).

Historically, men's writing has been used to construct objective reality, whereas women's has been condemned as too "subjective" for such a function (Miller, 1991). Having been shut out of publicly recognized writing projects, many women turned to diaries. Such autobiographical texts can be "sites of struggle where the subordinate can engage in contested relations with the social interests that attempt to subordinate them" (Fiske, 1994, p. 197). Smith (1993) claims that autobiographical texts provide a space within which women can "speak the unspeakable," articulating the fragmentary and marginalized experiences evacuated in the service of creating the illusion of the unitary self. While it is understood by many that this written self is merely "a strip of pavement over an abyss" (Woolf, quoted in Benstock, 1988, p. 1151), the process of reading and writing diaries still creates a different, more complex interiorized self. Psychologists Wiener and Rosenwald (1993) describe diaries as providing a transitional space to contain emotions and bind experience in time and charting development and change. Here an author can "see" herself and her experiences in a nondissociating way.

While these theorists and researchers have contributed to my thinking about Hannah's diaries, they often presume the author's capacities for symbolic thought, her abilities to know herself and her motivations, and the transparency of language (Riessman, 1993) to convey "reality." Unconscious motivations and desires are seldom discussed. Instead, diary content is used to piece together a coherent narrative of a life. There is little focus on the process of the text—what the patterns of content might mean or how the structure of the text may or may not have changed over time—or the impact of trauma on psychological functioning as reflected in the text. Here I attempt to demonstrate integration: I take what I have learned from the analysis of power and culture on the creation of subjectivity in anthropology, sociology, and feminist criticism, with the deep understanding of intrapsychic processes in the creation of relational psychoanalytic subjectivity, to explore the many layers of potential meanings of Hannah's text. As Trinh (1989) notes, all we have of the "truth" are stories. This book tells only one of many possible stories about Hannah's diaries.

Relational analysis has typically focused on psychoanalytic processes with people. Here I am stretching the theory to describe my relationship to a text and to a person, with whom I interacted primarily through a text. But analyzing Hannah's diaries was similar to analyzing a person. For instance, when Hannah writes, "Weighed and 107.6—really fluctuated from 107.1 down from 110.4 but I am 101.2 on scales at home (103.4 naked here). I have tried to tell the hospital—Emma and Dr. A—so it's up to them." I responded to the text as I would to a patient—with a wall of anxiety and the recognition of the feelings of power, powerlessness, control, and resistance that abound. Proud of her weight, Hannah shows off her control in the text then flippantly gives her responsibility to the doctors. Does she believe they will help her? (Why is she whining so much about her weight? Aren't there much more important things going on in her life? Why am I still hungry?) I fear that she could not seem to hold on to herself except through weight, which she seemed to use as a benchmark of her temporality from moment to moment. I am angry that the therapists might not be helping her enough, while I wonder if she is a demanding patient. I feel such frustration that in the middle of the diaries I am sick of hearing about how much she weighs all the time, bored reading weight figures, and tired of competing with her ability to deny herself food.

Using these gut responses to speak from, as Ogden (1989) recommends, I was forced to wonder about the different potential functions for what initially seemed to be a mundane symptom of her bulimia: compulsively weighing herself. Was weight a way of competing with others? Was my boredom an indication that when Hannah focused on weight her entries were suddenly deadened, void of affect? Was this the function for her, to void herself of any affective experience? Her shifts from problems with Eric to her weight and back again contained a certain mesmerizing rhythm that lulled me into a stupor. Could that be a function, to wring out anxiety from her life?

Weight functions on another level as well. Reading through the adult diaries, I was plunged into a world where I did not know what day, week, month, or year it was until I asked Hannah herself during the collaboration. At times I did not even know if the events were happening to her. I cannot overemphasize how disruptive it is not only not to know where you are in the world physically, but not to know when days end and others begin. The simple circadian rhythms are absent. Weight seemed to function quite literally to ground her (and me in relation to her text), to help locate her body by creating a particularly concrete form of space and time.

After months of living in this chaotic world, I was in an intolerable state of merged confusion. Gradually I began to realize that Hannah's inability to create any other form of time and space was her continuity. I began to understand that I needed to focus on her survival, even when it appeared self-destructive, and her resistance, even when to do so seemed complicit, for these were the cracks of space available for the creation of her subjectivity. Hannah's seemingly self-destructive behaviors around weight and bulimia actually were the spaces where she appeared. So, following Hannah's lead, I focused the analysis around her acts of resisting abusive relationships by creating her own time and space.

Using clarifying examples from her diaries, the next chapter provides the theoretical anchor for this book. The diaries themselves are front and center after that chapter. Chapter 3 explores the first two adolescent diaries, covering the years 1977 and 1978. Chapter 4 focuses on Hannah's last adolescent diary, 1979. Chapter 5 outlines her story as it was represented in her adult diaries. This outline is necessary if we are to contextualize the analysis of her chaotic adult diaries. Chapter 6 follows the first five adult diaries, and chapter 7 covers diaries 6–11. Chapter 8 has to do with the evolving structure of Hannah's text throughout these adult diaries. This chapter also explores her final two diaries, comprising almost exclusively lists. In the final chapter, Hannah speaks for herself, discussing the areas that she felt were most important to her transformation. But just as asking her to write her responses was a negotiation, asking her to speak for herself was also not so straightforward.

This analysis reflects Hannah's diaries. The chapters covering her adolescent diaries are organized chronologically because there was an external time of the date books in which she wrote. The exploration of her adult diaries is organized primarily by theme, following the ways in which she emerged in relationships with Eric, her bulimia, her body, and herself as she began to create her own forms of temporal linking.

Last, although my relationship to her diaries can seem like a relationship to a person, remember that this book is a diary analysis, not a case study. It contains descriptions of important clinical issues and illuminates ways in which psychoanalytic theory can shift and grow; but it is an analysis of a text, not a person, which means there are different spaces of constraint and freedom.

Chapter 2

The Anchors to Hold One's Self

Your tears they tell me
There's really no way
Of ending your troubles
With things you can say.

—Nick Drake, "Time Has Told Me"

Temporality was merely an interesting intellectual exercise until I entered Hannah's diaries. There, without the protection of my familiar sense of time and space, I began to understand our frightening dependence on such fragile constructs. Time is our continuity. It makes the "agonizing sense of the infinite" (Grotstein, 1993, p. xiii) consciously experienceable by creating minutes in hours in days, and an internal sense of going-on-being. Our capacity for time is a developmental milestone without which nothing goes forward.

There are many different theories of time (e.g., Merleau-Ponty, 1962; Bakhtin, 1981; Fabian, 1983; Ricoeur, 1984; Bruner, 1990; Kristeva, 1996; Thomas, 1996). Most link it to patterns of narrative language or meaning-making. Lakoff and Johnson (1999) describe two basic structures of cognitive temporal meaning-making: metonymic (cause and effect) and metaphoric (motion and resources). They hold that spatial motion involves the metaphoric orientation where the past is behind us, the present is where we stand, and the future is ahead of us. This orientation requires that either time is moving or we (the observer) are moving. For instance, in the diaries, Hannah often plays with time by propelling herself into what she imagines will be her future (observer motion) or by pulling the future to her by planning what she will discuss during her next therapy session (moving time): thus she is able effectively to avoid anxiety in the present.

Time is not only narrative or cognitive, however. Merleau-Ponty (1962) observed that time emerges only in our interaction with the world, which means it is inextricable from our notions of space (Lakoff and Johnson, 1999). Here time is an embodied creation, it "makes narrative events concrete, makes them take on flesh, causes blood to flow in their veins" (Bahktin, 1981, p. 250). As such, time and space are embedded in the very concrete, embodied relationships of power from which language and meaning arise (Kristeva, 1981). Therefore, we need to explore time as it emerges from both intrapsychic and cultural spaces.

In this chapter I integrate Winnicott's (1970, 1971) theories of psyche–soma development with one of the only psychological theories of temporality, Loewald's (1980) temporal linking. Although Loewald's theories of differentiation and symbolization are wrapped up in time, he often alludes only to its centrality. I am putting it front and center, within a cultural context.

Timing Cleavage and Differentiation

According to Loewald (1980), time initially is held and conveyed by the "mother"[1] in her rhythms and patterns of satisfaction and

1. Most developmental theorists conceptualize only the mother–infant dyad. Discussing them I will use this terminology, otherwise, I will refer to the "caretaker," referencing the primary caretaker, knowing there may in fact be more than one and they may not be identified as female.

frustration. The infant's "capacity for" inner reproductive holding emerges from these rhythms (Winnicott, 1971). The creation of a "capacity for" is the foundation of development and for going-on-being. Hopkins (1997) describes capacity as roominess, to have "room for," a simultaneous taking in and creation of. Thus, capacity is more than mere interiority, it is an actively functioning space of complex negotiation, where self and other simultaneously come into being.

This "capacity" contains experiences and enables the accumulation of a held past. Present perception emerges from this held past. Thus, the ongoing responsive patterns of this mother–infant dyad create and continue to modify internal experience as internal experience creates and continues to modify perception. Each new interaction is "shot through with memory" (Loewald, 1980, p. 157) from previous experiences, and each successive internalization reincorporates previous experiences, altering the past. This mutual building of perception and memory is a "product of the meeting between mind and world" (p. 157). Foreshadowing Butler's (1990, 1993) notion of subversive repetition, Loewald contends that memorial activity is a process of *recreation* similar to digestion, which transforms food into energy. Here all forms of perception, retention, internalization, and anticipation are also always elaborations and integrations, such that no perception is exactly the same, yet no perception is entirely new. One is continually engaged in the process of recreating one's past and thus one's present self.

This process of creating memory is inextricable from the experience of separation from and loss of the mother. After all, if there is no differentiation between infant and mother, there is no need for the creation of memorial activity. Without frustration there is no impetus to internalize or hold satisfaction, but without satisfaction there is nothing to hold on to. Memorial activity involves a fine balance, in that differentiation is gradually produced only as memory emerges, and memorial activity emerges only as differentiation begins. The process of memory is necessarily boundary generating, differentiating inner and outer, self and other. This memorial aspect of time is not only the "fiber" of the psyche

(Loewald, 1980, p. 52), for, by being a bridge, it actually creates the capacity for differentiation.

For instance, when Hannah is married to Eric, he tells her when and how much to eat. As she notes, she cannot always remember what she likes, when she is hungry, or how much to eat. As long as Eric remembers for her, she never needs to remember; but until she can remember, she needs him or someone else to remember for her. They must function as one undifferentiated body.

Ideally, we are continually moving between experiences of oneness and differentiation, and it is this motion, this capacity for a paradoxical process (Ghent, 1992) that plumps life with meaning. Thus, temporal linking is the continual attempt to recreate oneness through differentiation without separation.

Internalizing Memorial Processes

But how do the rhythms of maternal care actually become internalized? To fill in this theoretical gap, I must turn to Winnicott (1960, 1971). Winnicott (1971) conceptualized a spatialized environment that includes both the infant and mother within a limiting membrane of oneness. The rhythm of "good-enough" responses from the environment enable the creation of an elastic stretching and contracting bubble of predictability and expectation that is contained by the limiting membrane. Within this bubble, the infant is able to create a continuity of being and stability that is the basis for the creation of temporality. This holding environment is itself a melding of physical and psychic holding, for the mother holds the infant with "that aspect of her that remains not identified with him, . . . she makes her presence known in an unobtrusive way" (Hernandez and Giannakoulas, 2001, p. 155). (Even the mother's mind, her psychic thoughts, must be "good enough.") Thus, the "capacity for" (Hopkins, 1997), the functioning space of meaning making and reflection, is initially conveyed in both the mother's mind and her bodily holding, indicating that the limiting membrane is itself an integrated psyche–soma. As the environmental responses tenderly and "unobtrusively" frustrate the infant, the limiting membrane gradually wraps tighter until, equated with the surface of the skin, it incorporates only the infant self and defines an "inside and outside body-scheme" (Winnicott, 1970, 1971).

This complex process of differentiation requires the use of transitional objects. A transitional object is imbued with the goodness and badness of the environment, thus, it functions as an externalized capacity for meaning making that holds the infant together psychically while she is literally *"in transit"* (Green, 2001), neither inner nor outer, neither self nor other yet, but moving toward them. This transitional object is created by the infant, as she alone imbues it with projected intentionality, but it is also out there to be found. The specific rhythms of arousal, satisfaction, and frustration with the mother will be projected onto the transitional object. The presence of the transitional object indicates that the infant is in the process of incorporating the holding environment and moving toward the creation of "inner reproductive holding" (Winnicott, 1971) and an internal experience of going-on-being.

That is one way of conceptualizing the function of Hannah's diaries as they become a container of her undigested, unsymbolized experiences. Through them, she is able to hold complex and at times even contradictory responses. For instance, before she can bring it up in her therapy or to Eric himself, she tests out an idea by wondering whether Eric actually does know how much she should be eating. By asking this question only in her diaries, she keeps it in the transitional realm, where it is and is not her thought, where she can try it on, write it, read it, but not fully integrate it until she is ready. She and her diary, in this sense, can function as one psyche–soma within one limiting membrane.

Temporal Links of Faith

Being able to "use" (Winnicott, 1971) the transitional object and develop the capacity for memorial processes requires not only the accumulation of "good-enough" responses, but also the creation of temporal links. Here the current experience of arousal must be linked with past experiences of arousal that themselves resulted in satisfaction. Thus the infant is able to travel through time—

from present experiences of arousal to past experiences of satisfied arousal and then into the future—by creating an expectation of satisfaction. In the diaries, Hannah uses this cycle of time by creating plans for her future to pull herself out of a current state of arousal into a place where her anxiety-provoking situation has been resolved. This is self-regulation based on temporal linking that creates a time and space in motion.

According to Loewald (1980), temporal linking places all perception within a temporal context, where there is a continual recursive relationship with past, present, and future, between arousal and past satisfaction, creating a present of hopeful expectation. This linking renders experience experienceable by providing the necessary context of continuity, that is, time. It is time that creates the limiting membrane, the psychic skin that holds the integrated psyche–soma and differentiates inner–outer, self–other. In so doing, it holds the mind–body together in the face of the annihilation of conscious existence. Thus, temporal linking, memorial processes, and capacity for become inextricable processes, continually cocreating continuity and going on being.

The very concepts of expectation and continuity entail a leap of faith that the future will, in fact, mirror the past accumulations, that the rhythmic timing and spatial proximity of the object will continue uninterrupted and in a predictable manner. Therefore, if Hannah is anxious about being away from Eric, she can pull the future toward her by imagining what it will be like when he returns; but doing this will work only if she can accumulate past interactions where he has returned and use them to predict when he is likely to return. Hannah must take a leap of faith each time she creates a future from her past experience. Although Buechler (1995) and Mitchell (1993) have written of hope in psychoanalysis, I think faith is different. According to Webster's II (1999), faith is "belief in the *value* of someone or something" (italics added). Hope is "to want or wish for with a feeling of confident expectation." Hope implies a "preconception" of a particular future (Mitchell, 1993), a particular endpoint. Faith, as I am using it, is more amorphous. It is a leap from nothingness into uncertainty (Kierkegaard, 1980), where the *value* is in the leap, the process of making meaning in the face of nothingness, not the particular meaning that is made.

Here, the infant's or Hannah's particular expectation may indicate hope, but engaging in the process of creating that expectation itself requires the capacity for faith. This capacity does not imply believing in something; it is belief in the *value* of believing: faith in believing and finding a pattern to the rhythms of arousal and satisfaction; faith that one knows what to do to get a response from the environment; thus, faith in connection, faith to anticipate future interactions from the past that transforms discomfort in the present. This faith is integral to time's functioning. It enables time to be not only a linking activity (Loewald, 1980), but also a container (spatial capacity) holding the collection of past experiences from which the "leap of faith" to anticipate the future can be made. This "area of faith" (Eigen, 1981) creates the capacity for illusion. It is the space that imbues transitional objects with function and timing, imbues a teddy bear or a diary with the capacity to soothe.

Faith spatializes time, first by creating an interior space of accumulations from which meaning can be generated (the functioning space I have been referring to as "capacity for") and then by pulling time into the social realm by creating relational connections. Simultaneously, time binds faith; it provides shape through a trajectory, such as the future of "going-on-being" or the accumulated past. Without faith, nothing could be held as dear, nothing would be worth holding. There would be no space between self and other, no object use, no transitional phenomena, no inner–outer. Instead, the strangling notion of certainty would collapse all distinctions in the desperate avoidance of the unknown. Time does not function creatively without faith.

The importance of temporal linking cannot be overemphasized. If a moment is not temporally linked, fragmentation and loss of the capacity for meaning making can occur. This process is not necessarily linear. For instance, a perceptual moment may be created by its link to a past moment (which is itself then recreated by virtue of being linked to this particular moment in the present). But both these moments may also be linked to a particular future moment. Temporal linking can occur in many different directions simultaneously, but the capacity for linking needs to be maintained. Thus, meaningful time is not based on a particular shape of direction (i.e., chronological time) but the spatial capacity for linking. When I describe Hannah as "collecting" events in her day within an entry, she is able to write chronologically, but she is unable to create temporal links making meaning of these events.

Timing Secondary and Symbolizing Processes

> Ever since man has learned to give each part of the body a name, the body has given him less trouble (Kundera, 1984, p. 40).
>
> Words are but the shell, that we ofttimes break our teeth with them to come at the kernel (midwife Sharp, quoted in Harvey, 2002, p. 328).

As the foundation for meaning-making, temporal linking is also the basis for secondary process and symbolization. According to Loewald (1980), language is present in life from the very beginning. During the developmental era identified by primary process, the infant is literally "embedded in a global, dense, undifferentiated experience" (Mitchell, 1998, p. 831) of language as sound. Like the flow of milk that the child takes in and transforms into energy, language and speech are taken in, digested, transformed, and given back. It is through "the mother's mirroring interpretation and organization of the child's urges, feelings, and actions" that "links of action and feeling become links of meaning" (Loewald, 1980, p. 169), that is, temporal links. Secondary-process meaning, then, signals the developmental era when the semantic elements of language are identified (Mitchell, 1998), and this meaning emanates from flowing, interacting temporal bodies.

For instance, when the baby experiences discomfort, a parent covers her with a blanket. This cause-and-effect experience of being cold then warmed creates a temporal link of discomfort with a parent's action of putting on a blanket. The word-presentation "cold" emerges from this action. The word contains the temporal link between primary and secondary process, and it is meaningful only to the extent that it is embedded within a space of timed interaction and conjures up the past experience of being cold and then warmed. Thus, an idea becomes an idea only when it is reinserted into an embodied context of meaning. As Mitchell (1998) noted, language provides the "life-enriching link between past and present, body and world, fantasy and reality" (p. 834), but only as long as language can contain and convey the emotional relationship within which the word was initially made meaningful. Secondary process, then, is not defined by the use of words, but by the ability to temporally link words and embodied perceptions. Verbal language is merely the container for a temporal link. Without this linking to plump words with vitality, one cannot engage in the "creative use of language" (Loewald, 1980), and words become hollow or dead.

Temporal linking provides words with the capacity to bridge primary and secondary (presymbolic and symbolic) processes. Words invoke the experience in its absence; they "render them present in substantial actuality" (p. 202). Words, like transitional objects before them, become meaningful only when they are embedded in temporal sensory memory and when we can create temporal links conjuring up that activity in mind and body. Necessarily, then, words also reawaken the relationship within which they were learned and first used and understood. Thus, the particular sensory experience of the caretaker–infant relationship is crucial and shapes temporal linking as well as symbolic meaning making.

Loewald does not necessarily privilege secondary processes over primary (Mitchell, 1998). The embodied, musical aspects of language in primary process ideally feed the temporal links of secondary process, creating poetry, "creative uses of language." "The meanings of the words and the sounds of the words as spoken create an interplay that generates experiences that are both cognitive and sensory—embodied understandings" (p. 838). Hence, one does not "advance" from primary (presymbolic) to secondary (symbolic) process; these developmental eras are actually "coterminous modes of experience" (p. 843). This conceptualization shifts developmental theory from being a linear progression first of primary and then of secondary (or presymbolic to symbolic) to being a recursive process, where both developmental times are continually in the process of reshaping the other. Within this recursive cycle of development, self-regulation and the ability to organize experience emerge within the capacity to temporally link states of intolerable affect (present) to satisfaction (past and future) spaces of inner to outer. This development rests on embodied time.

Creating the Capacity for Culture

Loewald (1980), and Mitchell's (1998) reading of him, helps create such an elegant relational theory. But, as often happens in psychoanalytic theory and clinical practice, they leave the mother/caretaker–infant dyad in a vacuum, where all meaning that is made, all temporal links, are limited solely by the capacities of the participants and never by those of the surrounding culture. For instance, when Hannah writes that Eric tells her she is hungry, we can see that he is identifying and labeling an experience "hunger" for her. But, unlike an attuned caretaker/partner, his use of this label is based on the timing of his body alone. He is not helping Hannah differentiate her experiences of hunger from her experiences of cold; he is further confusing her by projecting his hunger into her. But when she goes out into the world, this confusion of her hunger is reinforced by a culture that strictly regulates women's appetites and bodies in particular. Just consider psychoanalysis' foundational interaction of breast-feeding: it is a contentious act that is mandatory for one generation, vilified for the next, and always publicly regulated. We must ask how cultural projections might be internalized along with the mother/parent's flow of speech?

Minding Bodies

> "I 'know your name'."
>
> And so she stopped, afraid. If this were true, she would be trapped. Naming meant power. Adam had named the animals and the animals came at his call (Winterson, 1985, p. 142).

Loewald (1980) locates language as the bridge between enlivening primal density and primary and secondary processes. Even though this language is most certainly embedded within its original embodied relational context, it is still language that is the magic link—language contains the "power of life" (Mitchell, 1998, p. 835). What about the power of life conveyed in the embodied primary-process-era interactions of the mother/parent–infant dyad (see Kristeva, 1980; Harris, 2005)? Does the mother's body become colonized in the secondary process? And what about music, dancing, or other forms of nonworded temporal linking? Can these also create a "higher organization"? In Hannah's diaries it is not the words she writes that seem transformative; it is the way she writes, the structure or body of her prose. Why, in such a beautiful theory of integrating primary and secondary processes, does Loewald (1980) consider primary-process, "regressive" activity (body) compared with secondary-process thinking (mind)?

It is odd that bodies in particular become subsumed within each temporal link, being merely an ingredient of the links, while the linking process itself is a minded activity of language. The body breathes life into linking and secondary process, but only from a safe distance, after it has been carefully organized, minded, and named. The body here takes a position similar to how I see many current theories of symbolization (Freedman, 1985; Bucci, 1997), mentalization (Fonagy and Target, 1996, 2002), and self-regulation (Beebe, Lachmann, and Jaffe, 1997), where it functions as a vessel for energy discharge and self-soothing, enabling the mind to do its work. The role of the body parallels that of a good secretary (female), who deals with the details (trouble) so the boss (male) can carry out the vision unfettered. Loewald (1980) may acknowledge the embeddedness of bodies in language, but the language in bodies remains unexplored in his theory.

It is never an innocuous event to split mind and body, even in theory. Such a split always involves processes of privileging and gendering (and racing and classing) the rational mind (male) over the irrational body (female) (see Suleiman, 1985; Dimen, 1989, 1991, 1997; Butler, 1990, 1993; Flax, 1990, 1993; Goldner,

1991; Bordo, 1993; Probyn, 1993; Grosz, 1994, 1995; Aron and Anderson, 1998; Weitz, 1998; Dimen and Goldner, 2002). This rational, autonomous mind maintains its existence only by locating the "trouble" of irrationality and emotional dependence within the body. Psychoanalysis perpetuates this system, for, even though it is acknowledged that most of experience slips through the cracks of verbalization, words continue to be the prized currency. This privileging of words is apparent in the very naming of experience as symbolized and presymbolized, where presymbolic experiences are typically located in the body, while symbolic contains abstracted verbal forms, organized linearly in space and time. It is a goal of psychoanalysis to bring presymbolic experience into symbolic awareness, unconscious into consciousness, (embodied) enactments into (disembodied) verbal discourse. Thus, the very activity of splitting organizational processes into discrete, hierarchical categories of verbal–nonverbal, intellect–emotion, canonizes a gendered process of sacrificing the (female) body for the supposed unity and superior functioning of the (male) psyche. The male, minded category emerges unhindered by such "troubles" as gender, race, or class.

By minding temporal linking, minds not only bind bodies, they become the purveyors of time. As Loewald (1980) writes, time is a "product of the meeting between mind and world"(p. 157). Here individual minds dispense time, which splits not only minds and bodies, but time from space. Splitting time from space enables time to surface as a disembodied psychic activity (Grosz, 1995). In the absence of an acknowledged (and valued) experience of space, male-identified bodies construct an "artificial" (p. 121) world where the production of knowledge depends on the violent erasure of space—bodies, "femininity." This splitting also obscures the relational nature of time. Time enables social interaction, and social interaction imbues time with meaning (Garrett, 1996). Time is not merely the "fiber of the psyche" (Loewald, 1980), it is the fiber of embodied relationships. It is through time and space that differentiation becomes a new form of connection.

Timing Trauma and Dissociation

The clinical relevance of this discussion deepens when we are dealing with trauma, where the very structure of the abusive situation is one of subsuming, objectifying, denigrating, and, as a response, sacrificing embodied awareness for a minded one. Dissociation is a normal process that enables us to narrow our awareness when we are overstimulated (Bromberg, 1998). In severe trauma, this narrowing excludes huge sections of experience and compromises safety and psychological continuity; in other words, it alters the capacity for temporal linking. Without temporal linking, experience is left floating, unlinked and unguarded by succession, anticipation, or other forms of temporality, and therefore continually retraumatizing. Disrupted time shatters faith in the existence of patterns and leaves a survivor completely adrift, with no sense of where she or he ends or begins, what she or he desires, and thus that much more susceptible to others' meaning-making. With no temporal linking there can be no self-regulatory activity, and without self-regulation there can be no differentiation, and with no differentiation, there can be no symbolization. It is a fragile developmental house of cards. Without meaning-making temporally linking psyche–soma, the mind and body are left to fend for themselves. The body often becomes the site of attempts at regulatory processes through self-mutilatory behaviors and relational enactments, not so much to reenact, but, because, in the absence of a capacity to accumulate meaning, repetition may be the only meaningful pattern conceivable.

Without temporal linking, trauma must be dissociated and held in the body for the survival of the split-off psyche. For instance, Hannah describes feeling sick and flinching when Eric touches her sexually. Her experience of sexual intimacy is not only occurring in the moment with Eric, but also in the past with her abuser. She is having two simultaneous experiences, but one is located in her response of flinching, as her body "keeps the score" (van der Kolk, 1994) as a "memory pad" (Bourdieu, quoted in Hoy, 2004), holding the past in "safe" (i.e., out of conscious awareness) keeping. This reliving in the moment indicates a disruption in temporal continuity; Hannah is in at least two different times and spaces simultaneously yet in neither as an experiencing, person. As the past infects her present, Hannah finds herself responding inappropriately to both. This response disrupts the present event further, rendering it even more disorienting and disturbing. *[Hannah: allergy to chlorine]*[2]

Such reliving behaviors can be seen as reenactments of the original trauma (Davies and Frawley, 1992, 1994; Aron, 1996; Bromberg, 1998; Layton, 1998). Davies and Frawley (1992, 1994) have outlined a structure that these enactments often take, acting out complex interactions between the embodied memories of the child, adult, adolescent, and parent personas. The memories of the trauma are literally embodied by a child persona. This child persona is the collection of embodied memories of abuse and the body on whom the abuse was perpetrated. The child is hidden away so that the adult persona can survive and thrive. The adult exists only because she has dissociated the child victim. When the child threatens to surface, a fighting adolescent emerges to communicate the trauma of the child in the veiled language of enactments, for instance, through the development of bulimia. These enactments allow the victimized child and the abusive parent to reenact the abuse on the body, out of the conscious awareness of the adult. The different patterns become catalyzed in relationships with others, and often the others with whom they are relating take on an opposing persona.

Certainly, when I describe Hannah's diaries as a chaos of time, events, and people, this is one way of understanding the confusion.[3] Hannah may begin an entry bingeing and purging as the angry adolescent; shift into the guilty child requiring punishment from her husband; embody

---

[2] Hannah remembered that she developed an allergy to chlorine after being molested by the school priest in the pool area of her school. It was at this point in her reading of the analysis that she linked her allergy to this experience.

[3] Material set in sans serif type is my analysis that Hannah thought was particularly moving.

the rescuer, who understands how self-destructive it is and who says she will never binge and purge again; and then shift into the competent adult by describing her work successes [the "carer"].[4] In one entry she is able to play out roles of being the victim, abuser, and rescuer. And these shifts may occur within one short paragraph, so that each sentence is literally a separate, unintegrated, undigested moment in time, written by a different facet of her self. These shifts are occurring continuously on many different levels, usually out of conscious awareness.

While this structure is helpful and obviously translates to this analysis, it is important to remember that, again, these shifts are dynamic and cannot be pinned down simply and neatly. Reenacting trauma is not just enacting roles and behaviors, these enactments are continually reshaping and reorganizing self-experience. And because survivors typically cannot integrate and reflect on themselves (Bromberg, 1998), even within repeated enactments, each experience seems to "just happen" and there is no capacity for accumulation or meaning making. Hannah collects situation after situation where sex "just happens" with various men, with no sense of cause and effect, beginning or ending. It may be the reenactment itself that provides the only way in which a survivor may hold herself through time. While these enactments may shift, they continue to provide the organizational structure for attempts at temporal linking. [√][5]

Dissociating Gender

Now, to backtrack a bit: If the body holds and communicates memories of abuse, then the surviving competent "adult persona" (Davies and Frawley, 1992, 1994) is free to succeed in the work-

---

4 Hannah called the rescue persona the "carer" because she thought this aspect of herself cared for herself.

5 Hannah also created a scale of checkmarks to indicate sections that she thought were particularly important. As she stated during the collaboration, "Most parts are spot on, but some are really on." She marked these sections with one to three checkmarks, three signifying the most important. I have included these checkmarks in italics in brackets *[✓]* at the end of each paragraph she marked. Using the same symbol better respresents how she chose to participate in the analysis and represent her voice within the text. These are the sections that most moved Hannah.

world unhindered by embodied memory. What remains unspoken in this setup is that this competence is being mastered in a specific space of the white patriarchal public world. Thus the adult persona is not just any adult, but a white male or male-identified persona: a persona devoid of an experiencing, "troubled," female body. Here the survivor of trauma succeeds by becoming a male adult playing by male adult rules (repudiating emotional, physical, and interpersonal desires) in the white male adult world, while the gendered female victim remains victimized in the private female world. This process, gendering experiences, spaces, and time, forces female and male victims once again to abandon some connection to their identified "female" self in order to survive. Here it is not only that as "females" they were victimized but that as "males" they will survive. And, if the abuser was a male, they are not only identifying with the abuser, they are becoming him.

In other words, this theory of traumatic reenactment is dependent on the gendered stereotypes of public–private, adult–child, and perpetrator–victim.[6] So when Hannah is starving herself, she is not only reenacting the abuse of her child persona while acting as an impulsive adolescent quelling the screaming child, she is erasing her decidedly female body (starving off her hips and breasts), which was abused as a female body in the female private realm by (in her case) two males and a female. She is perpetuating the killing off of her female self that she tried to kill when she originally created a male adult to replace the female child. And, by creating this male adult she is also siding with the aggressors, who are identified as male for their power to victimize. There are multiple levels of not just self-abuse, but specifically misogynist self-abuse, and as Harris (2005) notes, the corresponding multiplicity of personas, time, and space are equally gendered. Gender can be "available and malleable for many different forms of psychic work, including the metabolizing of trauma" (p. 147), as Hannah's diaries demonstrate. [√]

---

[6] Exemplifying the impact of gendering spaces, males who kill partners within the domestic sphere receive much lesser sentences than males who kill strangers or other people within the public sphere (Heberle, 1999). This reflects sanctioned male power within the private sphere as well as the lesser value placed on women's lives as victimized domestic property.

Minding Dissociation

Even the concept of dissociation itself must be temporally linked to the culture. Heberle (1999) points out that early in the family violence literature "patriarchal terrorism" was used in favor of "domestic violence." Patriarchal terrorism is a more inclusive descriptor, as it identifies the gendered violence that resonates throughout the social structures within and outside the home that condone and perpetuate male violence against women and children. By shifting from this term, we create a privatized notion of violence that is seen as the result of dysfunctional family dynamics and individual psychological pathology. The misogynist culture is erased. This shift also enables psychoanalysis to become the purveyor of "normality," pathologizing culturally unacceptable behaviors as dissociated traumatic repetitions (see Haaken, 1998), enacting what Harris (2003) describes as "a psychoanalytic account [that] too easily privatizes psyche and leaves unremarked the material historical conditions and social practices that maintain misogyny and make use of it" (p. 259).

Identifying temporal linking as a cultural event provides a way to conceptualize dissociation and traumatic response that incorporates these material conditions. Here we can identify the limits of the cultural discourse (not the individual psyche) as responsible for rendering experiences unlinkable. This more expansive idea of temporal linking recognizes that forms for making meaning are based on a very limited repertoire of gendered, raced and classed narratives (see Gergen and Gergen, 1993) that will necessarily leave certain experiences unspeakable and that this cultural limit itself is a site of trauma and traumatic repetition.

Situating temporal linking culturally also helps illuminate the fact that, even when narratives are available to organize experience, they can traumatically shape the experience. For example, sexual violence against women is the one violent crime where victim-blaming remains the most common form of meaning-making (temporal linking) for both the survivor and the community (Lamb, 1999). Here, cultural ideals of gender and sexual responsibility cocreate a particularly limited, retraumatizing, and dangerous temporal cause (the victim's behavior) and effect (sexual violence) through which to make meaning of trauma.

When Hannah is suddenly grabbed and kissed by a taxi driver as he deposits her luggage in a hotel room, her only response is to ask herself what she did to ask for it. Her behavior is central to the temporal linking, whereas the perpetrator's/taxi driver's is normalized or condoned by inattention. As Ferenczi (1933) noted, the victim is retraumatized when the experience of the event is not publicly and relationally recognized, and, here, the limits of socially validated narrative forms (i.e., temporal links) as well as their particular content (i.e., victim-blaming) add additional levels of trauma.

Focusing on temporal linking also helps illuminate where victims resist. As is described more thoroughly in Chapters 6 and 7, resistance need not be conscious or spoken, for it, too, can exist and be enacted within unspeakable spaces. When Hannah binges and purges after an abusive or controlling comment from Eric, it is clear that she is simultaneously identifying with him/the aggressor by becoming the abuser of her own body and attempting to regulate her affective response; but, in doing so, she is also resisting his invasion. She is dominating her own body, getting rid of it once and for all on her own terms. These intentions may be unconscious, but they are still forms of resistance. So focusing an analysis on the many layers and forms of temporal linking can be quite fruitful.

Linking Dissociating Bodies

> There is no way of authentically capturing the horror of abuse, except from the first person, from inside the skin. It is no coincidence that this perspective is precisely the one that is most devalued and distrusted in our culture [Rice, 1996, p. 226].

Bodies link what cannot be heard within the narrow spaces of culturally constituted, psychoanalytically valued verbal discourse. As Rice notes, trauma may disrupt certain forms of temporal linking, but other, equally significant forms of linking may be established. The pervasive effects of trauma are not only linked to the organizational capacities of the psyche, they involve the cultural processes out of which the capacity for temporal linking emerges.

Time provides a unique potential space within which to reconceptualize trauma because temporal linking emerges from the meeting of bodies, minds, and cultures (Loewald, 1980). Thus, the capacity for, the space of meaning-making that creates an interior, is actually a relational construct that is both inner and outer, intrapsychic and cultural. This conceptualization, then, locates trauma relationally, not only in the abusive incident, but within the cultural space that (dis)embodies language and cocreates the "capacity for" temporal linking. This shift is imperative for evolving theories and treatments of trauma and eating disorders because it enables us to see that behaviors identified as self-destructive reenactments in the clinical setting may actually be resistant and life-affirming on the cultural level. Thus, creating the space to explore the many relational and cultural meanings is necessary and must be kept in "mind" as we delve further into Hannah's diaries.

Chapter 3

There's No Safety in Numbers

As noted in the first chapter, Hannah's adolescent diaries focus primarily on friendships at school. Therefore, the focus of this and the following chapter is on the evolution of her friendship group as represented in her adolescent diaries. The growth of this group is tracked by how Hannah describes the patterns of her friendships. In other words, it is not only the content of her entries, but the geometric patterns of pairing, breaking up, and merging again, that tells the story of her friendships.

Here I introduce and track the movements of Hannah's friendship group from 1977 to the middle of 1979. This group generally functions like Bion's (1959) "basic assumption group." Bion delineated three relational forms around which such a group organizes. The dependency group is marked by the presence of a distinct leader around whom the others congregate. The support and faith of the group members turn this leader into an omnipotent and omniscient leader who provides hope and meaning to the group in many different ways. In the diaries, the hostess of a party can become a leader who provides an event to look forward to and plan for months in advance. All members will defer to her about whom to bring, whom to date, and what to wear. Of course, this exclusive power sets the leader up for a coup. If the leader even hints at failing, there is rebellion and another leader is established.

A second form is fight or flight. Here fighting or fleeing a common enemy or against an emotion or thought serves a cohering function, uniting the group members in an action-oriented task of avoidance. It is not the object or person being avoided but the act of avoidance that serves the cohering function for the group. The third type of group is created when members pair. Bion likens this form to two Messianic leaders who have emerged to lead the group to a utopian existence of cohesion. The pair creates hope for the other members to cling to avoiding their own experiences of hatred, anger, or frustration at one another. These forms of relating are not exclusive as groups slide from one to another depending on the predominating interpersonal needs. All three types are relevant to Hannah's friendships.

Within a culture that limits potential experience on the basis of race, class, sexual orientation, and gender, group dynamics undoubtedly take specific forms with a gathering of possibly all white, upper middle-class, seemingly heterosexual female adolescents. I say possibly because Hannah never mentions physical descriptions. She describes two of her friends as having boyfriends, but it is unclear what that means for their sexuality. They are disembodied names on the page. This absence of bodies is described further in the next chapter, but, suffice to say, in the diary of an adolescent female in Western culture, it is interesting that appearances are absent.

Aggression, however, is not absent. Some research contends that females have different ways of relating within relationships than do males (Brown and Gilligan, 1992). One main component of this difference is females' tendency to avoid anger, disagreement, and conflict (Brown and Gilligan, 1992; Harris, 1997; Brown, 1998). This avoidance results in ways of communicating anger that employ relationships more than verbal dialogue through which to articulate the anger (BjÖerkqvist et al., 1992; Hadley, 2003, 2004). This observed difference in communication has been identified as indicating girls' "indirect" communication of anger and use of "manipulation," relational meanness, excluding people, and backbiting versus boys' "direct" communications of anger (BjÖerkqvist et al., 1992).

There are many problematic aspects to bifurcating and gendering these communication styles. First, categories of gender and sex are culturally produced, and thus are less than reliable in explaining behavioral differences. Second, as mentioned previously, psychoanalytic theory privileges direct communication as a sign of health over other forms of embodied dialogic communications. Obscured is that communicating "directly," regardless of the context or relational implications, requires and assumes social privilege. Those in power can speak their minds directly because it is most often what those in power speak that defines what is speakable in the culture.

Third, male physical violence is identified as a direct and normal expression of aggression (e.g., "boys will be boys") whereas female relational violence is identified as indirect manipulation, yet both effectively express a message through pain and humiliation. Furthermore, boys, too, manipulate and girls also fight physically. Girls are physically violent, but their violence often falls under the radar (Ness, 2004; Raghavan et al., 2005; Rajah et al., 2005). It often remains "unseen" because girls' violence does not usually result in the same level of physical injury or property damage that male violence can lead to, and, as described previously, it challenges our notion of the female gender role. Aggressive girls are "catty," and if they fight it is a "catfight." The cultural definition of female is not wide enough even to include the potential for aggression or violence, so females are linguistically changed into cats.

On the other hand, "female aggression sets off irrational social and intrapsychic anxieties" (Harris, 1997, p. 297). For instance, women receive much longer sentences for equivalent acts of domestic violence than do males (Heberle, 1999), despite the fact that oftentimes the partners whom females kill have established records of domestic violence and the women have failed orders of protection. Here the culture can also respond to female aggression with an iron fist, sending the clear message that, even if you are being abused and threatened, don't you dare get angry, retaliate, or defend yourself. It seems that girls' "indirect" modes of communication may be the safest and most effective, as other forms are liable to be dismissed, ignored, or punished.

Hadley (2003, 2004) has reviewed the research on girls' aggression, little of which deals with physical violence. This research details a female underworld of name-calling, teasing, social ostracizing, gossip and backstabbing, stealing girlfriends and boyfriends, and forging and destroying social ties, all with a big, innocent smile. Given our pervasive stereotypes about gender and aggression, however, it is unclear when girls are acting toward agency, assertion, creation, or in retaliation (Hadley, 2004). It is difficult to say whether they are recreating a patriarchal hierarchy, struggling to fit into a violent world, or being "good" girls who would rather compete for the meager resources doled out to young women than organize collectively to topple the system.

Additionally, we need to consider how these limited avenues for expressing aggression affect girls' psychological development. Harris (1997) contends that familial and cultural systems do not teach females to metabolize and digest their aggression. Indeed, while boys have sports with rules and referees to aid in the exploration of their aggression and competition, girls have grades, clothes, and dieting—in essence, their bodies as the field to compete on. There are no referees; there is no external containment. Without the relational tools necessary to digest and symbolize the experience of aggression, it remains potentially overwhelming, as it cannot be broken down, chewed up, and used to create meaning. These undigested self-states then become dangerous, avoided, and disavowed. Anger and aggression then become relational hot potatoes, more potent tools for potential manipulation. This transformation is only amplified by the extreme responses of the culture to female aggression.

Within this cultural atmosphere and without the relational tools to metabolize aggression, many different feelings can become conflated such that women often cannot distinguish among feelings of ambition, destruction, and anger (Harris, 1997). Additionally, because our culture condones males' use of violence as a form of differentiation (Hadley, 2003), girls are stuck with few capabilities to experience a full range of aggression or differentiation—the latter, as described in the previous chapter, being necessary to the development of temporal linking capacities. Not surprisingly, then, all these feelings can become identified with aggression and are experienced by girls as dangerous to friendships. Brown (1998) goes further to contend that any extreme emotion can be experienced as dangerous and requires quelling within female friendships. The analysis of Hannah's friendships seems to exemplify both contentions in that expressions of extreme emotionality, competition, ambition, and aggression are dangerous within the friendship group.

Blocking the Friendship Scene

Hannah's adolescent diaries begin when she is 14 and living just on the outskirts of a small town an hour outside London. As mentioned in Chapter 1, these diaries are date books, which for the first two years provide only seven lines per day for an entry. She fills these lines with detailed accounts of other girls' interactions from school. It is unclear who these girls are to her, how she feels about their fights, or what exactly her role is in those fights. There is no introduction to the girls, who they are, and what a typical day comprises. At first, Hannah does not seem to have any particular friends, until gradually Tina and Meg and then Karen emerge. These adolescent diaries are the introduction to Hannah and her world, yet she really appears only as a reflection of how she tracks her friendships. She does not appear in the text in any direct way with the pronouns "I" or "me." Indeed, my initial response to reading her first diary was that she seemed to be walking through her world as a robot with no insides, that she collected quotes from others and pinned them on to her shell in an attempt to create some sense of a self. *[Hannah: She doesn't feel]* [1]

---

[1] Responding in third person, Hannah wrote that she did not feel at this point in her life.

In an attempt to provide a more helpful introduction to Hannah and her life in her adolescent diaries, I am outlining the four basic rules that stand firm in her friendship group.

Rule #1: There is no discussion of needs or bodies. It is socially unacceptable to be identified as having desires. Instead, you must position relational interactions in the way that will most likely result in your getting your needs met, or you must wait patiently until someone offers to meet them. As she states, "Meg has spread round that it is my birthday tomorrow. It is a duty of a friend!" Hannah cannot tell others it is her birthday; she must hope her friend will speak for her in the group so that she will get a party and gifts. Given the recursive nature of subjectivity and desire described in the previous chapter, such a construction of not just indirect but passive communication of needs must contribute to significant alienation from one's needs, desires, and body. If you are lucky enough to have a friend who can read your mind–body, you might not have to split off your needs, but if you are not that lucky, dissociation of your desires may be the only way to be a gendered girl in this group. Either way, it is a tenuous form of embodied existence. And with no needs comes no bodies. As mentioned, girls are here in name only. There is no discussion of appearances, clothes, or even the spaces they inhabit. If females do not develop the capacity to express themselves and their aggression directly, they are set up for a dangerous relational cycle with men. Relational forms of communicating require complicity, in that the other must know the unspoken rules. Hannah walks through a world where her "indirect" or relational ways of communicating are often quite effective with her female friendship group. She is able to get what she needs on some level. With men, however, her relational communications are fairly ineffective. When she is being pursued by a young man who is writing her love letters, she writes, "Wrote short letter back. Hope it puts him off," and when another tells her he wants to marry her, she says, "Said nothing, I hope he understood." She is unable to tell either young man, "Please leave me alone." And, predictably, these tactics are not effective. They set her up for a dangerous cycle, where she is speaking almost a different language from that of the males while trying to communicate her needs, limits, and boundaries.

When relational maneuvering does not result in getting her desires met, they are disavowed, experienced as illegitimate. This disavowal creates a relational cycle with others that has a simultaneous intrapsychic cycle of splitting off embodied desire and leaving Hannah more vulnerable to and dependent on outside forces to identify her "internal" desires. This cycle of the simultaneous creation and disavowal of female desire is elaborated throughout this book. [√]

Rule #2: Friendships are for couples only. As Hannah tracks friendships she creates a ballroom dance viewed from above, couples swirling in circles, continually changing partners. *[Hannah: I like analogy]* Like a ballroom dance, the steps are made for two, and three throws off the rhythm of the friendship, calls into question the original alliance, and forces a choice by one of the girls to revert back to the coupled format by choosing either the new friend or the original friend. As Hannah states, "It seems ok when I'm alone with anyone, but when there [are] two of us [two others along with her] no matter (nearly always) who the two is, things then go wrong." So the stability here is in the structure of friendship (two people) and not in the alliances themselves (between the particular people). *[Hannah: same as triangle at home]*[2]

Rule #3: Despite all the fights and messes, Hannah's hands stay clean. Hannah charts changing alliances like a cartographer, concretizing and nailing down social interactions. But Hannah is watching from the balcony above. There is no mention of her having a connection to these events or people. She is not dismayed, upset, or happy about anything. However, she does convey emotion through the language she chooses to map this dance, where "breaking up," "dumping," "going round with," being "chucked," "dropped," or "leaving" someone are the makeup of daily school life. "Kara dumped Tina for Sue; Ruth dumped by Rose for Sally; Tina wants to dump Kara for Ruth, but Ruth dumped Tina for Rose and Sally." Ostensibly, since she chose the verbs to write; these dramatic descriptions locate her participation and subjectivity in the friendship dance. And these descriptions convey a notion of romantic love gone astray, rejection, and abandonment.

Rule #4: Friendships do not last. Friendships appear to be a frightening combination of tenuous and unpredictable passion. For instance, friend-

[2] Hannah said her family was the same in that she could relate to her mother or her father, but not both simultaneously, and they both related primarily through her.

ships cannot withstand any conflict or differences. Meg and Tina do not get along because they have "different ideas on life," and Hannah and Ruth cannot be best friends because Hannah did not understand something Ruth said. Kara can go from Tina to Ruth to Sue to Tina without a blink. The bonds of friendship are tenuous, not only because of their temporal instability, but because there is no incentive to maintain bonds; friends themselves are easily replaced. [√] *[Hannah: same as with men now]*[3]

Hannah anonymously charts the movements of the group for months until gradually she writes only of her own interactions with Meg and Tina. In this chapter, I focus on the evolving relationships with these two friends because it is in these relationships that Hannah begins to write herself into the story.

Introducing the Perfect Pair: Meg and Hannah

- Had a row with Meg about Sue.[4]
- Had a row with Meg cos of Ruth. She is so bloody possessive.
- Meg jealous yet again about Tina and I. Put it down to a mood!
- Tuesday is always the worst day for rows with Meg and today certainly lived up to its reputation. Normal theme, Meg's jealousy over Ruth.

Despite Hannah's lament about troubling triangles, tales of three-way friendships, not couples, dominate these adolescent diaries. In the majority of triangles, Meg is the consistent member with Hannah. Their relationship is easily the most tumultuous in the adolescent diaries because Meg, with her disruptive "moods," is cast as the eye of each social maelstrom. As Hannah writes, "Spent lunch time with Kara and Sally as Meg was in a mood with me." Not only is Meg moody, jealous, and demanding of Hannah's attention, she is also drawn as being spontaneously open about expressing aggression not only within her "moods" but within her brutally honest opinions about others. For instance,

---

3 Hannah said this is how she currently relates to men.

4 Bulletted comments represent separate excerpts from Hannah's diaries.

- Meg went off in a "huff" at lunch as she said I talked too much to Ruth about "silly things"
- Had a row with Meg about Sue. Meg says she always tags along and cries crocodile tears
- Meg is getting bored of routine and called Tina a wet sponge
- Had a huge row with Meg and sat with Ruth and Karen all lunch. Eventually Meg rang me up and said sorry after saying we would break up forever

As the only group member who voices opinions about others, Meg seems to be the voice for the group. She says what comes to her mind regardless of the consequences. She instigates fights by accusing others of being fake; she walks out if the conversation is not to her liking and says so; and she tells people how she feels about them even if it is negative.

Despite Meg's seeming openness, throughout the text, Hannah expresses her concern over whether Meg is trustworthy. When Meg gets her menstrual period, Hannah says:

- Meg "started" on Sunday and so at moment is in with Tina. She told us but not Lynn (or so she says!). Lynn away again ill with "a cold," or so Meg says. Funny how she always seems to have a cold every month!

Hannah fears that Meg lies not only about which friends are having periods but also about who else has been told about who is having her period. Meg tells her that Hannah is the only one she tells, but Hannah questions this professed fidelity and automatically creates a third point on the triangle. This attention to periods also hints at the importance placed on the bodies of these developing young women, for Hannah's mistrust of Meg here refers to whether the group members are being honest about their status as menstruating or nonmenstruating bodies. These diaries, however, track the menstruation only of other girls—there is no mention of when or if Hannah begins menstruating. Her body is absent.

The ultimate mistrust or betrayal occurs when Meg visits Hannah's house, and she writes "Walked home and later Meg read my diary. Really bad and now can't trust her." Meg cannot even be trusted in Hannah's room as she found and read her diary. However, it is in this example of distrust that I become painfully aware that Hannah's response to this transgression is no different from her response to the other descriptions of mistrust. She does not seem to differentiate between the different levels of personal-boundary transgressions from potentially being lied to about someone else having her period, watching Meg lie in school to a teacher, and having had her diary invaded. Each is discussed as representing the same level of distrust. [√]

The mistrust between the girls must be palpable, which leads me to wonder where Hannah is located in this relational space. How is Hannah trustworthy? I know from these entries that she does not seem to acknowledge her own feelings to Meg. "Meg in bad mood with me as says I never tell her anything e.g. Wales" and "Meg found about Tim, hence Colin." Here it is Hannah who does not tell Meg she is going to Wales with Sue, nor does she tell Meg she has a boyfriend named Colin. So it seems Hannah fears that Meg tells her lies but all the while she herself is withholding information from Meg, and Meg gets in a mood over it. Perhaps this withholding creates a cyclical pattern of Hannah's making Meg feel left out, which contributes further to the overall relational feeling of tension or mistrust and jealousy on the part of each of them.

Yet despite (or because of) this seemingly high level of mistrust, their friendship seems to thrive. As Hannah states, "Meg getting much closer again and saying how we are much better friends now than then." However, as this quote demonstrates, this is Meg's opinion, not necessarily Hannah's. Hannah does not write her opinion.

The Wonder of Triangles

Hannah struggles to relate to Meg in a pair, but, in the end, most of these diaries are about triangulated relationships. Indeed, triangles enable Hannah to relate to others while controlling relational contact with them and with her own emotions. She can easily split and project her indigestible experiences onto others. Triangulating with Meg seems to serve a variety of important relational functions for Hannah, including regulating conflict, competition, and emotional responses, and helping Hannah find her role as a peacekeeping friend.

Triangulation as Conflict Resolution

- Today, tomorrow and Wednesday broke up with Meg! Lynn not here but she will go round with her and me with Tina and Karen. Meg seems part jealous of me because I'm not going to crawl back and Tina and Karen are on my side not hers. Meg has seen that I am not bothered and like Karen and Tina better than her. so is talking quite normally to me. Meg being terribly nice lately—says us two still leaders of group.

When the leaders split, the group itself splits and some go with Hannah and some with Meg. But Hannah's understanding of the conflict is that it can be resolved by jealousy and she brings in a third relationship for Meg to observe. Meg sees that Hannah is not bothered by their conflict and, in fact, is relating to Tina and Karen, who are siding with her. Here the geometry is three-dimensional, as Hannah adds Karen and Tina to create a triangle on her side, while Meg adds Lynn to create a triangle on her side. The presence of these others serves primarily to solidify the importance of the pair. The triangulated relationships may be with Tina and Karen, but Hannah is watching Meg's behavior first and foremost. In Hannah's entry, her use of Tina and Karen is successful, and Meg begins to talk to her again.

Then another conflict ensues as Meg attacks the entangled third in their triangle during school. Hannah writes:

- Meg got detergent bottle and went for Karen. Karen squirted it all down Meg's back. Meg got told off for running out of the room but said it was Karen who soaked her.

Here Meg attempts to attack Karen by squirting detergent at her, but it is Karen who succeeds in soaking Meg. Meg is identified by the school authorities as the misbehaving student and is punished. With two points in the relational triangle fighting each other, Hannah is drawn to Meg when she gets in trouble. So it is as if another triangle is created through the presence of the school authorities, and Hannah sides with Meg.

Within the group, conflict resolutions emerge from the physical activity of including a third party and not through a verbal discussion of feelings or experiences between Hannah and Meg. The girls cohere by playing out their conflict within the group. Such forms of resolution are typical of the basic assumption group that lives with little or no sense of the self-awareness necessary to discuss conflict verbally (Bion, 1959). By dealing with conflict relationally, however, the group is also behaving appropriately for their class and gender. Perhaps it is not only a lack of self-awareness that maintains their level of functioning, but the knowledge that following culturally appropriate gender-role behavior trumps personal awareness for women.

Triangulation as Competition

Meg "pairs" with Hannah by saying the two are "leaders of the group," which has complicated consequences. Certainly, it bonds Hannah to Meg through their special leadership mission. Identifying Hannah as a leader also differentiates her from the rest of the group and potentially compromises her relationships with others, pulling her closer to Meg. But this pairing also creates competition between Hannah and Meg for control of the group. However, Meg does not compete directly with Hannah, instead she enlists others to do it for her. As Hannah writes,

- Meg thinks she is Tina's friend over their shared secret "It's about time someone beat Hannah over something: Keep up good work at physics, Tina." Quote of Meg, from Tina.

Meg plans to use Tina to dethrone Hannah by having Tina get a higher score on a physics test. Using Tina serves multiple purposes. First, Tina and Meg do not really get along, but, by supporting and complimenting Tina as the only person able to beat Hannah, she forges an alliance with her. Second, although this alliance is based on Tina's pairing with Hannah as the two best physics students in the class, Meg simultaneously pairs them and divides them by planting the seed of competition and resentment between them: "It's about time someone beat Hannah over something."

Third, dethroning Hannah and replacing her with her own friend would constitute a multiply layered coup. Hannah would no longer be at the head of the class, and her bond with Tina would be jeopardized. Meg then could step in to become the one and only friend for Hannah, who, no longer at the top of the class, would not be a threat for control of the group.

Unfortunately for Meg, Tina tells Hannah. This move strengthens Tina's bond with Hannah by disturbing Hannah's bond with Meg. Not only does Tina dash Meg's plans, but she lets Hannah know that Meg, supposedly her friend, is planning a coup. By doing this, Tina instigates her own triangulation, as Hannah's relationship with Meg has been a bone of contention for her. Here multiple triangles fold in on themselves, creating a tumultuous mess—Tina upset at Hannah for her relationship with Meg, Hannah upset at Meg, Meg upset at both Hannah and Tina, and Hannah the center of another triangle and still the recipient of the highest grade in the class.

Triangulating to Be the Peacemaker

- Ruth was in a sad mood today because Rose is going round with Sally. I tried to cheer her up but it didn't work.
- Spent all general studies consoling Sue and keeping the peace between her and Joan.

Within these triangles, Hannah often has the role of consoling others. She not only cheers up people, she also places herself, or becomes placed, between fighting parties. She takes no side but is important to both. But who does this placing? When Hannah finds out that Ruth has dumped Tina for Rose and Sally, she says, "Of course, guess who has to tell Tina?" Whether she took it upon herself or was asked to do the deed, she takes on the role and by doing so strengthens her bond with Tina by telling her the news and comforting her. Simultaneously, Hannah also strengthens her bonds with Ruth, Rose, and Sally, by doing the deed for them. Thus Hannah comes out with four strengthened social alliances by acting as the peacemaking voice for one breakup.

This example demonstrates the complexities involved in taking on the role of peacemaker. Whether others place Hannah in this role, she takes it on herself, or, more likely, it is a complex group interaction, Hannah derives multiple benefits from being put in the middle, and as with any form of triangulation, the maintenance and strengthening of alliances comes only at the expense of others' relationships and alliances. [√] *[Hannah: watching mother's body language]*[5]

But acting as the peacemaker within these fighting pairs creates and maintains a situation where resolution occurs only through the activity of complex relational communication. She talks to each partner of a pair and explains the other's behavior, and by talking to each partner she "sorts them out." The partners do not speak directly to each other about their feelings or conflicts. Instead, Hannah steps in to act as the interpreter, providing an explanation to both parties. This is a specific relational mode of conflict resolution that may help the group maintain its pairs and some semblance of cohesion. Given that Hannah has described difference alone as ripping friendships apart, her role as the peacemaking interpreter is probably imperative for the group to continue to function. *[Hannah: no discussion allowed]*[6]

But this role of the peacemaker provides Hannah with a slippery subjectivity within the group. That subject is based on her not having a response to events and instead acting as a vessel to channel other people's communications. According to Renik (1995), nonresponsiveness is often experienced by others as ambiguity, not neutrality. So, when Meg has a big birthday trip planned with the group, Hannah is not included. As she writes:

- Heard from tactless Meg. [that I]had been discussed, and Lynn and I found unsuitable. I asked why. (1) [I] never argue so they don't know where [I] stand.

Here Hannah is getting feedback from Meg about how others in the group experience her social neutrality, her refusal to take sides. They evidently experience it not as peacemaking or peacekeeping but, rather, as disturbing. They are not able to know where she stands on things and they would rather she not accompany them on a trip. [√√]

---

[5] Hannah said she had to assess her mother's moods at all times because her mother was so labile. Hence Hannah became hypervigilant about reading emotional states and being a peacemaker in all situations.

[6] She said there was no discussion or resolution of conflicts at home.

But this peacemaking role is complicated. Does Hannah have deep responses to others that are withheld from them perhaps as conflict avoidance? Does she have these responses but dissociate them? Does she literally not have the capacity to create responses? At times, Hannah writes of having strong feelings, but these are not shared with the group; at other times, things happen and she writes as if she were an objective, uninvolved court reporter. It seems that Hannah's capacity to create experience and thus to relate to others is severely constricted. Sometimes she seems to have no sense of her own experience, whereas at other times she is overwhelmed by it. But at no time does she share her feelings and responses with others. On one hand, she seems to disappear in relation to others like sugar dissolving into water, but, on the other, she exerts a powerful but invisible force to move people relationally like a poltergeist. [√]

According to Bion (1959), the person who subverts conflict can keep members from having to experience tension and anxiety, and that person will initially be welcomed by the group. Eventually, though, this peacemaker will be blamed for the group's not being able to work through conflict. This peacemaking member will have to take on a different role or be eliminated from the group. When Meg tells Hannah that the others do not know where she stands on issues and hence do not want her included on group activities, this is an indication that the group is entering a new phase of development where they are ready to have conflicts and resolve them. But, to have the opportunity do this, they must stop the peacemaking activities, that is, the triangulation. Consequently, Meg steps in as the voice of the group to warn Hannah that her role is no longer sought. Hannah will have to enter the group as a subjectivity with her own distinct responses.

Triangulating to Contain Emotion

Unfortunately, triangulation is well ingrained for Hannah; she not only reports triangles in her diaries, she also actively creates them each time she interprets Meg's or Tina's respective behaviors as indicating their jealousy or competition. In other words, the relational form of triangulation is how Hannah creates cause and effect; it is the shape of her temporal links.

For instance, Hannah and Tina seem to be paired by the group because of intellect; they are often the high scorers in the class. This pairing is reinforced by the group, who evidently try to calculate Hannah's and Tina's grades. As Hannah writes, "Told everyone me 81% and Tina 80% to stop them working out our averages which I hate." Offering their grades is an interesting response. By doing so, Hannah binds herself closer to Tina within the group—she knows Tina's grade and demonstrates that she knows it by telling it to the group. She and Tina are so close that Hannah can speak for Tina. And their grades are close numerically, differing by only one point.

But this binding also serves a competitive purpose. Hannah may be sick of the girls' calculating their grades, but she chooses to tell the scores of a test on which she just happens to have the highest grade. She answers the group's call for pairing and ups the ante by competing with her selected paired partner, Tina. This interaction is particularly important because, although Tina and Hannah seem to be paired by the group, Hannah indicates that she is not taking on this pairing role entirely. Through a competitive triangle of her own construction, Hannah creates a space for her desire, which is to beat Tina and end the competition. But this desire only peeks out, being held and conveyed within a complicated, triangulated form of relating.

As described in Chapter 2, all temporal links are relational, but here we have an example of such a link in the absence of the "capacity for" creating them internally. Instead, Hannah, externalizing her temporal links onto the page, moves others around like chess pieces, to embody split-off parts of her internal experiences. Meg and Tina feature largely in this function.

It is apparent from Hannah's descriptions that Meg and Tina contain different kinds of emotions for the group. Meg has been pegged as the voice of the group; she says what is probably on everyone's mind. She is drawn as a loose cannon, uncontrollably expressing herself like a raw id, running through the world on impulse. Hannah identifies her as "tactless," but Meg is also the only one who seems to be able to express difference. Not surprisingly, Hannah's relationship with Meg is marked by the tension of fights, blowups, social coups, backstabbing, and friendship, all calculated maneuvers with no emotion. When Hannah is enlightened to Meg's scheme for getting Tina to best her in physics, she writes "Got physics test back got 64% and beat Tina who got 53%." Period. No gloating or comment, even in the diary. And when Meg and she break up, Hannah creates many different relational maneuvers.

- [I will go around] with Tina and Karen. Distinct improvement on my part but Meg seems part jealous of me because I'm not going to crawl back.

To every action of Meg's there is a reaction from Hannah, but there is no elaboration of the processes through which Hannah comes to these responses or how she actually feels. *[Hannah: compete or avoid]*[7]

This absence of emotional response in relation to Meg becomes even more apparent in contrast to her interactions with Tina. Tina is the container of emotion. She gets "upset" and must be calmed and soothed. Unlike her calculated, action-oriented responses to Meg, Hannah's discussion of conflicts with Tina involve descriptions of emotions. For instance, when Hannah is asked on holiday with Sue, her first response is, "The only trouble is—do I tell Tina, as I don't want to deceive her but also don't want to hurt her?" When Tina finds out about her trip with Sue, Hannah writes, "Tina made me cry and she did too because of holiday in Wales. Better now as broken the ice and stopped us both concealing our feelings. As long as nothing is ruined."

This is a radically different interaction from the one Hannah described with Meg. Not only does she worry about hurting Tina's feelings, but, when she does, they both cry. This is the first of two expressions of Hannah crying in the adolescent diaries, and both occur when she is relating to Tina. The other occurs when Tina is "very depressed and seems unable to be cheered up." As Hannah writes:

- They say the more depressed you are the deeper it becomes and it certainly seems like that is also catching. Had letter [from Tina] and when I read it I just burst into tears. I couldn't help it.

---

[7] She competes or avoids the situation.

Not only does Hannah cry when Tina cries, but she even "catches" her depression. She describes herself as being connected to Tina on an emotional level that causes her to react in a way that she has not described with anyone else in the diaries. For instance, contrast this description of Tina crying to that of Meg crying. First Hannah writes:

- Lynn said god, Meg you really are a bitch. I'm not surprised Tina gets upset. In fact, you are the biggest bitch I know. Ruth said [Meg] cried all afternoon. Does Lynn care?

Hannah sides with Meg on the last question by asking if Lynn cares that she upset Meg, but Meg's upset does not seem to upset Hannah, or she does not write it as such.

Even when Hannah is the cause of Meg's upset, Hannah seems to be able to maintain a distance, as indicated when she says, "Had a row with Meg over her meanness. She cried but I apologized though Karen/Tina said I was right." Here Hannah's comment causes Meg to cry; and, even though Hannah apologizes, it appears from the entry that she holds on to her self within the relationship. She knows she was right, if only because Karen and Tina thought she was right. Of course, that also could be an example of Hannah's bringing in Karen and Tina to triangulate, creating the relational distance necessary for her to hold on to what she thinks she knows in this moment about Meg: that she can be mean. But, regardless of the tactics, Hannah seems create a distance from Meg even when she is in relation to her. This relational distance is not found when Hannah is describing her relationship with Tina.

Relational distance seems to be integral to friendship continuity for Hannah. When she describes her and Tina's openness, she follows it without a breath by stating that there is a potential for ruining the friendship by such openness of feelings. As Brown (1998) found, strong feelings are potentially dangerous to female friendships. Additionally, unbridled openness increases the potential for recognizing differences. The one issue that continually threatens Hannah's relationships, especially with Tina, is lack of similarity:

- Tina says we are less like each other now. I've heard that one before and seen the results. Possible result obvious and not amiable.

Hannah identifies difference as being absolutely deadly to relationships. She has heard that one before and has seen the results. It is an ominous comment about the dangers of difference to friendships. To go back to Harris's (1997) observation, females are not taught how to deal with aggression and hostility, and without females' capacities to digest these experiences, differences become deadly. They cannot be worked out on a sports field, wrestled away, or contained by a referee. Instead, girls are forced to struggle alone, with no rules, no boundaries, no containment, and no cultural discourse—forms of temporal linking—through which to express, understand, or experience their aggression. It becomes an emotional *Lord of the Flies* (Golding, 1954).

Within this treacherous environment, Hannah can use others through whom to moderate relational distance, compete, communicate, fight, and, in the end, rebound. Through a third person, she can fight or flee her self-experience and the group dynamics. In relation to Meg's uncontrollably aggressive id and Tina's overly emotional one, Hannah can surface as the ever-rational manager ego. Such splitting not only helps stabilize the group, it also helps to regulate Hannah by enabling her to split and project her overwhelming experiences of aggression and emotion. Without Meg and Tina to contain these experiences for the triangle, Hannah might not be able to maintain the role of the emotionally devoid, rational, peacemaker. She might have "moods" too.

When Opposing Points in the Triangle Meet

Triangulation as externalized temporal linking becomes complicated when the objects of Hannah's triangles take on lives and intentions of their own and demand more contact. While interactions with Meg typically remain triangulated, Tina pulls for a dyadic relationship from Hannah. One way she does this is to attempt to contact Meg directly, usually aggressively, as a way of pulling Hannah closer to her. For example, Hannah details "black Monday:"

- I don't know which of us got out of bed [on] the wrong side but someone has a lot to answer for! At school K., L., H. [Karen, Lynn, Hannah] all talking and T.[Tina] walked in. I said hi to her but others didn't (well M.) [Meg] Things progressed and it seems T. upset as M. is "rude" Karen "amazed" at T.'s temper which annoyed T. even more!
  T. not speaking to M. At lunch M. and T. argued a little and K. and I went out. Later I had music and Tina wrote me a note. Read it and so did K. a little upset as feels she is odd one out. Reassured her (I hope).
  Came home and K. rang. Had dinner and rang T. [she] seemed happier.
  Rang K. and talked and then gave her T.'s number. Rang
  Meg. T. ok. Thank god.

Here Tina walks into the room and when only Hannah greets her she loses her temper at Meg. This conflict lasts all day and ends only after Hannah initiates five phone calls. As usual, the emotional fire is conveniently contained within one body, and the voice is neatly contained within one "tactless" person. But Tina and Meg are becoming very difficult angles for Hannah's triangles; the girls require more and more frantic peacemaking activities. Here Hannah must mobilize a telephone-brigade that includes Karen, in order to keep the threesome from (de)evolving into dyads of Hannah–Meg, and Hannah–Tina.

After this incident, Tina attempts to use Meg's transgression as a way to bond closer with Hannah over the idea that Meg is "rude." She writes a letter to Hannah describing her feelings about Meg's "rudeness." The letter gives Hannah reason to reconceptualize Meg as being a "rude" person; she perhaps puts their bond into jeopardy or at least shifts it slightly. Harris (1997) notes that women's fear of hurting trumps their fears of being hurt themselves. Tina plugs this fear of hurting into the relational matrix of Hannah's friendships to create the perfect recipe for retaliation against Meg. By emphasizing how much Meg has hurt her, Tina gains the upper hand in a way that is much more powerful than merely getting angry at Meg.

Meg's retaliation, a note of apology to Tina, is one of the most interesting uses of triangulation. Couched within her apology is the statement, "It's hard to be best friends with Hannah but the quiet times make up for it." Meg advertises her intimacy with

Hannah to Tina within the guise of an apology. This triangle gets deeper when Hannah then attempts to explain Meg's letter to Tina. Hannah tells her she "has no cause to worry (not a deep one. for Meg it is only superficial)" and that she should not be "upset over 'Meg and I.'" Hannah's attempt to make Tina feel more secure continues advertising her intimacy with Meg. She knows, or professes to know, Meg's innermost motivations: Meg is "only superficial." Hannah knows Meg on the inside as well as on the outside and is willing to explain her behavior. Tina responds by getting upset about Hannah's and Meg's closeness. It seemed that Tina was attempting to bond with Hannah and split off Meg once and for all, but Hannah's intervention strategically and relationally bonded her with Meg and placed Tina back in her corner.

Here again, Hannah's "peacekeeping" itself actually contributes to the maintenance of this emotionally charged triangle. Having fueled this split between Tina and Meg, Hannah centers herself within the triangle by constructing the theory that it is Tina's possessiveness that is causing the difficulties and that will push Hannah away as a friend. As Hannah writes, "If only Tina realized she is more likely to lose me by telling me she's worried and trying to keep me." So Hannah fuels Tina's insecurities by advertising her intimacy with Meg. Then she proceeds to give Tina all the agency and choice for ending or maintaining their relationship and absolves herself of having any impact on Tina's jealousy. "If only Tina realized," but who will tell her? Although Hannah is privy to this information, she cannot or will not tell Tina. [√]

Despite (or because of) Hannah's peacekeeping efforts, Tina's moods escalate. Yet in the diaries these conflicts represent an effect without a cause, as Hannah discusses only the fallout, never the conflict itself.

- Tina gave me a card and we apologized.
- Tina said "it's over. I'm leaving the group." We both cried and stood and talked in the rain. Tina not too bad, but now just take one day as it comes for the majority do not get too hurt that way!
- Tina was very bitchy whenever she said anything to me—Couldn't win—either saved her a place and she looked down her nose as if to say "I'll only deign to sit with you as nowhere else" or [I] didn't and she got in a mood.

None of these comments were preceded by a description of a fight or conflict, but the emotional fallout is omnipresent and located in Tina's "moods." With all conflict located within Tina and Meg as the product of some mysterious "mood," responsibility for resolution is also located exclusively in the other; and Hannah does not have to experience or own her responses preceding, during, or following the conflict. There is no cause and effect (temporal linking). Fights "just happen." But this disavowal most likely keeps conflict a frightening and devastating event. If conflicts are located exclusively in the other and have no identifiable cause and effect, Hannah is powerless to comprehend, resolve, or avoid them. This is one of the downsides to externalizing one's experiences.

Hannah and her friendships literally are psychically interconnected and interpenetrating. She lives off of them, they are her life blood. If she is not in the center of a relational maelstrom, Hannah may cease to exist, or she may have to experience her self. But as her peacekeeping efforts fan the conflict between Tina and Meg, each of their demands for fidelity from Hannah also escalate. As Tina and Meg each vie for a monogamous relationship with Hannah, Karen steps up to take the role of chum, leading Hannah into a dyadic relationship. [√] *[Hannah: no trauma?]*[8]

---

[8] Hannah was surprised that there was no discussion of the trauma going on at this time. Evidently her reading of this analysis was multiply layered as she was filling in the absences as she went along. This example of multiple simultaneous self-states is discussed further in later chapters. Her comment also indicated that she did not remember what she had written in the diaries. She had not looked at them for years before she gave them to me.

Chapter 4

A Primer of Self-Destructive Rituals for Becoming a Woman

- Meg says anything which has to be worked on that much [as much as Hannah's relationship with Tina] isn't worth it but then she probably believes in divorce unlike Karen and I.
- Chatted to Tina and said I would sit next to her [the next year]. Told Meg at break. Lost her temper and cried a bit but apologized afterwards. Meg changed my decision and I let Tina down. Told her and she took it very well for which I must admire her. [W]ished Karen had been there, still I suppose I have to make my own decisions.

In the previous chapter, we saw Hannah struggling to maintain ties to Meg and Tina through her role as the triangulating peacemaker. In this role, Hannah was able to control relational contact and distance with both friends by pitting them against each other for her attention. But it became apparent in the analysis of these diaries that Hannah needed these friends close by, for they served a containing function for her projected self-experience.

This chapter follows Hannah until the end of her adolescent diaries. The year is 1979 and Hannah has just turned 16. She is still struggling to maintain the balance between Meg and Tina. But, as their conflicts and demands escalate, Karen takes the stage to function as a crowbar extricating Hannah from within these triangles.

Karen becomes not only a school friend, but Hannah's first after-school friend. Their activities usually involve going to Karen's house to perform gendered rituals, such as dieting, exercising, shaving, putting on makeup, and painting toe and fingernails. Until now, there has been little to no mention of bodies, and there is no sense of anybody's appearance. Is everyone white? Who is tall, short, thin, heavy, pretty, blonde, brown haired? I have absolutely no sense of bodies or spaces here. This is an interesting realm of experience to be absent from an adolescent diary. Again, it seems as though there are multiple dissociated elements of experience that are played out in Hannah's friendships. In her friendship with Meg, Hannah is rational and calculating; with Tina she is emotional; and with Karen she is a physical body. Together they may form a "whole" experience, but this is a tenuous mode of existence for it is entirely dependent on the presence of another person to serve as a container. [√]

- With Karen am really glad I have someone I can be real with well as real as I can be.
- Really very close to her now, and can't imagine surviving without her! Amazing to find someone I get on with so well!.

According to Sullivan (1953), a chum is a close friend, a member of the same sex, with whom one develops an intimate relationship based on consensual validation. Such validation involves each person's supporting the experiences of the other. Through this mutual validation, a chumship can help correct developmental warps that the person has in relating to others. So a chumship can be a reparative relationship that furthers relational development. This reparative function is what differentiates a chum from a best friend. Indeed, here, Hannah's relationship with Karen is the most intimate and nontriangulated she has with her peers. *[Hannah: double dates, empathetic to her trauma and sadness]*[1]

[1] Hannah said she became closer to Karen because they went on double dates. She said she also felt sorry for Karen because her older sister had run away to London and committed suicide. This must have been quite traumatic for both Karen and Hannah, but neither of these connections to Karen is discussed in the diaries.

By March of 1979, they spend much of their after-school time at one another's house or meeting at the letter box between their two houses. The first entries about their friendship describe Hannah's letting Karen read her old diaries and Karen's starting a diary to let Hannah read it. That Hannah lets Karen read her diaries stands her in opposition to Meg, who read them without Hannah's permission. Hannah also places Karen opposite Meg, when she writes that Karen, unlike Meg, does not believe in divorce. There is an alliance based on a similarity of belief, and the content of this belief is the permanence of interpersonal bonds.

Within a relationally tumultuous environment where friendships are formed and destroyed and reformed within one day on the basis of a comment or a failure to greet another friend properly, it stands to reason that a friend who is similar, especially in valuing the permanence of relational commitments, will be invaluable. Similarity seems to signal a deep connection, without which a friendship is doomed never to be a "best" friendship. Although it is still unclear what exactly similarity is—is it being able to communicate differences without a fight or conflict, or is it a state of never communicating about differences and ignoring conflicts in favor of seeing only the similarities?—this element is integral to a best-friend relationship and to chumship.

The Bodies of Chumship

Hannah's chumship with Karen is the relationship that has the most impact on Hannah's socialization to the stereotypical female gender role. Karen is the first girl in these diaries who actively dates and worries about her appearance, clothes, and losing weight. Karen is Hannah's entrée into the world of "femininity" through specific rituals. *[Hannah: my hero]*[2]

Bodies take on specific cultural meaning through rituals that connect the individual body to the cultural body (Douglas, 1966,

---

2 Hannah touchingly described Karen as her hero because she was a model of what Hannah saw as mature femininity. Her comment perfectly illustrates this discussion of rituals' creating the female body through their capacity to temporally link to the cultural body.

1970; Turner, 1984; Martin, 1987; Synnott, 1991). For instance, rituals through which female bodies come into being within the culture involve cleaning (especially during menstruation), shaving, exercise, diets, makeup, girdles, bras, confining clothes, high heels, perfumes, concealing creams, colored nail polish, and the like. These rituals, which seemingly purify the female body, stem from and support the cultural ideology that women's bodies are not acceptable without constraint, modification, and sterilization. Through these rituals, one learns how to be a woman by objectifying the female body. Thus, ritual functions as a form of cultural temporal linking, giving the individual body a cultural space or capacity for making meaning. The cultural meaning that is made then cocreates individual experience. This experience, in turn, reinscribes meaning back onto the cultural body. The fiber of the psyche and interpersonal relationships is necessarily going to be shaped by cultural ritual and ideology, which itself is in continual flux based on shifting cultural needs.

Systems of power and ideology are sculpted in the very muscles and tissues constituting our bodies, so that each movement we make at once locates our bodies within a cultural hierarchy and reproduces that hierarchy (Sampson, 1996). The "trick" of these rituals, or pedagogies, is that they effectively obscure the (temporal) links between cultural control and the political ideologies reinforcing them (Bourdieu, 1977), between the emergence of the body and the ideological sculpting.

For instance, Nasser (1997) notes that economic shifts coincide with alterations in idealized body size, shape, and clothing for women. When the culture requires women to be at home and reproduce, an exaggerated ideal emphasizing the waist of the female body is sought—(for instance, the Victorian wasp shape, the postwar 1950s hourglass shape). But when the culture requires wide-scale female participation in the public sphere, the ideals shift to being thin, straight, and prepubescently "masculine" (e.g., the 1920s flapper; the svelte movie stars of the 1930s–40s; Twiggy in the 1960s and the progressively thinner, anorexic ideals in the decades since) (Seid, 1994; Wooley, 1994; Hesse-Biber, 1996). While there are other variables affecting this timeline (e.g., race and class, to name only two), fashion trends convey important messages about the role female bodies play in the culture at a particular time. Fashion provides temporal linking, meaning-making, for individual bodies to emerge within the cultural body. There is a correlation between women's access to public space and the amount and shape of embodied space they are supposed to take up (Hesse-Biber, 1996; Nasser, 1997). Through ritual, however, this controlling and misogynous political ideology masquerades as health, nutrition, beauty.

Many theorists link these changing restrictions on women to capitalism and media images (see Bordo, 1993; Gutwill, 1994a, 1994b; Orbach, 1996). It is also necessary, however, to emphasize that capitalism is merely one more ideological system of many that are organized around hierarchies of gender, race, class, sexual orientation, and the like. Certainly, the needs of a capitalist culture are met through discourses of medicine, fashion, and nutrition, which then dictate and patrol the ideals of gender, but as Nasser (1997) points out, historically, women's appetites have been controlled in preindustrialized settings too. Control of female appetites (whether to fatten up, lose weight, not have sexual desire, etc.) through cultural ritual is an old, pedagogical trick. In other words, the form that oppression takes (e.g., lose weight, gain weight, alter the body in some way) is based on the particular ideal that is peddled to women and men, and this ideal is related to the organizational needs of the culture. The source of oppression is not the form of the ideal, but the existence of an ideal, because such ideals are used disproportionately to control women.

Ironically, until this point in the diaries, Hannah has existed in a cultural vacuum. She seldom, if ever, mentions popular culture, music, television, or movies. Her hobbies are collecting antique hatpins, reading antique collector magazines, and attending Royal Shakespeare Company performances. Karen helps her create temporal links to a peer cultural body, and these become the only bodies in the adolescent diaries.

As Hannah begins creating a body with Karen, she also creates the space within which these bodies travel. This space, too, comes into being only in relation to Karen, as Hannah writes that they are so close now that they can see "each other's rooms in a mess and not mind." They can let it all hang out and see each other in states that no one else sees and still accept each other. They exchange clothing and razors, and they often sit on the bed in only their underwear and read each other's diaries and discuss crushes on boys. Bodies are all over this relationship.

Dieting Creating Self-Experience

Most of Hannah's interactions with Karen involve altering bodies, and dieting and exercise are the primary activities.

- Karen and I going on another one of her crack pot diets. I don't know why I agree to them—probably because if she is going to benefit from them and get slim so am I! This one is no chocolates.

Here is the first experience or expression of direct competition: Karen is not going to benefit unless Hannah benefits too. And this competition is in a stereotypical female space of dieting. In this realm, competition does not seem to threaten their relationship. In fact, it is followed by an exclamation point, rendering the whole endeavor somewhat exciting, or as she writes later, "fun!"

Creating this space for competition is very important. The girls in Hannah's diaries have no safe spaces within which to compete. Unlike many boys (and some other girls), they do not seem to play sports. Sports provide a safe, framed space within which to discover, explore, experience one's aggression and competition. There are rules for contact and referees to ensure that the play (fight) remains safe. A player does not have to worry about regulating his or her internal aggression in the moment. Playing in such a way creates a space within which to develop the capacity to experience one's physical and psychological aggression as potent, enlivening, destructive, and controllable. After all, our experience of space and subjectivity come into being simultaneously (Grosz, 1995). Emerging within a space of physically expansive activity—running, tumbling, getting dirty—acting on objects will create subjectivities distinctly different from those emerging within spaces of constraint, self-denial, and discipline of all appetites, that is, acting as an object.

Harris (2005) describes having joined a collegiate men's lacrosse team and how she became "entranced with the intense and particular cathexis of the athlete's body" (p. 134). This form of cathexis involves not just performing, as one would experience in individual sports like swimming, gymnastics, or ice skating, but the feel of the "impact of flesh on flesh, muscle to muscle," which she notes, does not occur for women outside of sex. The exhilaration of contact sports not only teaches the rules of competitive interaction, it unites body and mind in the pursuit of a cathexis of flesh on flesh. As such, it creates an alternative to the female body as the passive object of a male gaze. Instead, the female body has a competitive, forceful aggression with potency, boundaries and limits that are experienceable on impact. As Harris notes, it enables an experience of "function over decoration" (p. 134). It blows open the traditional boundaries of female embodiment where touching, walking, speaking, and holding one's body, hands, feet, arms, and legs are all premeditating and calculated to take up less space, where even holding one's own gaze must be measured in an attempt to control not only one's appearance to others, but how others will respond.

For Hannah and her friends, aggression is used only when it can be refracted in multiple levels of triangulated fighting, manipulation, and competing. Even Meg, the voice of the group, competes with Hannah primarily through the mind of Tina. Furthermore, Hannah and her friends compete all day long. There is no safe, identified, framed space within which to save their aggression and take it out later. And they compete about everything: grades, who the teachers like, friendships, who has a boyfriend, who has her period. There is no rest, no relaxation, no rules or referees to help them focus and contain their aggression. Instead, it is floating freely and constantly among each of them all the time. There is no safe experience of aggression, no chance to discover the creativity of aggression, no chance to know aggression as anything other than destructive.

Through dieting, Hannah can compete with Karen (and other women) and still maintain her connections, even, perhaps, strengthen them. Dieting provides rules, strategies, and rituals. It is a concrete way of competing with others without overtly stating the competition. And, like the space of sports, dieting provides a space of heterosexually "safe" contact. On the sports field it is acceptable for males to touch each other in ways that in other spaces would be considered (homo)sexual. Similarly, dieting with Karen creates an acceptable space of intimate physical contact within a heterosexist culture. Hannah and Karen sit on the bed in their underwear comparing their bodies. Rituals around disordered eating and bodily control seem to enable Hannah and Karen to experience aspects of their own sexuality, albeit only through the guise of dieting and in only those aspects that safely fit into a heterosexist culture. Dieting, however, takes the relational explosion of cathexis in physically aggressive sports described by Harris (2005) and turns it inward. Instead of cathecting against another body, one learns to cathect against one's own desires as if they were a foreign body for attack.

Hannah and Karen's first diet, described earlier, involves a prohibition on chocolate. So dieting is described negatively: what they cannot have. This first diet day is followed without comment by a day of eating her favorite cakes for tea.

- Went home with Karen and we had tea, shortbread, and Madeira cake which are both my favorites.

The second diet involves not only the negative but also the affirmative—what they can have,

- Karen and I decided to cut down on food especially chocolate to lose vital inches for summer. Decided to have orange and yoghurt regularly and not too much chocolate and fried foods.

That represents the first splitting of food into categories of what can or cannot be eaten. The intentionality behind the diet is that the girls want to lose "vital inches for summer." By the end of this day, Hannah has already eaten chocolate cake, and this time she mentions breaking the diet. But she seems to take it in stride as she says, "I'll live each day as it comes!" *[Hanna: Hardly!]*[3]

---

[3] Evidently, the happy-go-lucky representation of breaking the diet in

- Also had some lovely cakes laid out for me including a foreign one in choc.-oh dear, and it's 1st diet day and pastry from Holland. Still it was lovely . . . I'll live each day as it comes!

The third time they diet Hannah actually names the day "Diet day," literally setting it off from her regular life. The diet is described in the affirmative only—which foods they can eat.

- DIET DAY! Breakfast in bed–1/4 post and 1 banana milk shake . . . 2nd banana and another at lunch and 1/2 pint of milk. Started to feel a little hungry and Karen agreed her legs felt wobbly and generally drunk . . . At home had another milk for tea and went to see Mrs. W–made it worse as offered coffee and biscuits! Karen rang when I got back and I told her I hadn't broken my diet . . . Dinner–yes banana milkshake and went to bed on banana milk shake. The trouble is we will only make up for lost time tomorrow so there seems little point–though fun!

This diet consists of eating banana milkshakes and drinking milk for three meals a day. As Hannah insightfully predicts, they diet for two days and then gorge on nondiet food.

- Karen bought 10 Mars bars at lunch and we duly felt sick!

This stepwise progression is an outline of "how to" develop bulimia. It perfectly describes what has been discussed by many researchers and clinicians: the physiological effects of food deprivation are to binge (e.g., Polivy and Herman, 1985). Here Hannah and Karen begin by "innocently" shaving off certain foods from their daily menus. Then they continue to shave these off but focus on eating "diet" foods, splitting foods into two categories, "diet" and "nondiet." Finally they eat only the diet foods, and the diet itself becomes a completely different experience from everyday eating as there is no longer any incorporation of previous ways of eating. Dieting becomes an experience in and of itself that is completely split off from their former "normal" ways of eating.

By this seemingly simple process, they have altered the way they think of nourishment and taking in foods. Suddenly there is

---

the diaries may have concealed a more intense response that she filled in while reading this part of the analysis.

a self-imposed line drawn between certain foods, and those falling on the "bad" side just happen to be some of Hannah's favorites. By labeling favorite foods "bad," she is forever altering the sense of trust (assuming she had some to begin with) in her experience of her body's "knowing" what it needs and desires. For this to happen, there must be a split between "self" and "body," only the minded self having access to the truth, knowing what the body really needs. The body becomes a potential temptress requiring domination and dissociation.

As the defined "bodies" of the culture, women tame their bodies through a process akin to Sisyphus's futilely pushing the rock. As with Sisyphus, the goal is not to get to the top of the mountain or to attain the magic weight, it is to be perpetually engaged in an arduous, endless task. And, once taken with such a task, there is time for little else. This is the "beauty myth" described by Wolf (1991) where in one exists as a body endlessly engaged in the process of becoming but never being. [✓✓✓]

As Harris (2005) notes, development is a specifically temporal endeavor, always embedded within a historic moment, that will imbue bodies and minds with the categories and meaning necessary (temporal links) for subjective emergence. This historic perspective is extremely important when we are exploring the meanings of eating disorders.

As Bourdieu (1977) and Harris (2005) observe, we tend to see the body as natural or essential, and eating disorders have become a ritualized way of being a woman. Dieting functions as a ritualized pedagogical trick (Bourdieu, 1977), effectively obscuring the temporal links between cultural control and political ideology. Dieting is experienced and conceptualized as an individual decision or a desire to meet a cultural ideal. It is not identified as the response to a political imperative to control female bodies and maintain patriarchal social cohesion.

Identifying and exploring the quality of these temporal links enhances our understanding of the connection between the individual and cultural meanings of behaviors. Hannah's dieting is a multifaceted and paradoxical method of gender socialization. On one hand, it enables her to create the ritualized link between herself and others; as such, it is a "fun" thing she and Karen do together. It also links her individual body to the cultural body by providing a discourse through which she can experience her appetites as appropriately shameful, and it emphasizes the importance of regulating her body as an object of "scaled" measurement. It provides a culture-based organizational frame in which she can enact her gender through the distrust and control of her body.

But this organizational frame is as fragile as it is rigid. The diet rules can make Hannah not eat even when her legs feel "wobbly" and she feels "generally drunk," but they are easily "broken" when she is offered cake for tea. When the phenomenological experiences of the body are regulated by the organizational frame of the diet, wobbly legs become linked to successful restriction. They no longer signify a message to eat. Hunger shifts from signifying a state of intolerable physical discomfort to signifying one of potential weakness, a threat that might break the will of the dieter. The body and mind are split, such that the body becomes the temptress in need of control. But the minded self must also control or limit the environment to make sure to avoid all temptation and thus secure the diet self. She must be hypervigilant, for she is always on the verge of giving in, breaking the diet, the link that makes her body culturally meaningful.

Here feeding, what Winnicott (1960) described as being one of the primary organizing experiences for the self, becomes a site of struggle for self-definition, creation, and destruction, a place where desires and appetites are immediately experienced as dangerous and "bad." The body, the primary avenue for "knowing" the world, is distrusted and destroyed as dieting (self-harm) becomes not only normal but also a way of being a woman. Not trusting the body—the site of meaning—leaves you unable to create adequate temporal links and meaning. This leaves women more susceptible to letting other people define their world. It may leave women more vulnerable to abuse and manipulation, as they are handicapped in their capacities to make meaning for themselves. [√√] *[Hannah: feel diet TO self-harm]*[4]

So as Hannah diets, then binges, then diets again, she creates a cycle of dependence. With each diet she becomes more and more in need of an external frame to fill in for her body as a sight of meaning making. But with each binge, she becomes more and more aware of the tenuous nature of dieting as that frame. It is the very definition of an abusive relationship.

---

[4] Hannah emphasized the self-destruction of starvation. This analysis here is only responding to the content of these diaries, which focused on dieting as a chumship activity. A more complex analysis follows in Chapters 6–7.

The Neatly Tucked Letter

As mentioned earlier, when Hannah and Karen become chums, they immediately begin exchanging diaries. During one of those exchanges in June, Karen writes a letter to Hannah and tucks it into the back of her diary. Hannah does not find it until July. It is after she finds and reads this letter that her world seems to change drastically. The letter reads:

- I hope you won't find this for a while but I wrote it on the 9th June when I read this. I don't think you're a robot anymore. You're a person too and everyone else is just put here to test us now! (know what I mean!?) We'll survive—honest Hannah! Even if our lives turn out rubbishy we've still got each other to console! You'll find the right person I know and let's hope I've found mine (hope so). Anyway keep smiling—you can always convince everyone you're happier than them!
  Luv
  Karen
  XXX
  PS I understand—Honest![5]

This note is baffling and affirming. On one hand it conveys Karen's changing experience of Hannah. She describes her earlier experience of Hannah as being that of "a robot," but says now, "You're a person too." It is astounding that Karen, too, describes Hannah as a robot, just as I had. This description implies that, in fact, there has been a significant change in the way Hannah relates with Karen. Whether Karen became friends with Hannah because she saw her as more of a person or whether she became more of a person within their evolving chumship is unclear.

---

[5] The opposite page has a drawing by Karen of rainbows with a smiling sun and the caption: "a picture is worth a thousand words (even a wordless one!)" Many diary pages have little covers shaped like triangles that were slipped onto the upper right-hand corners of the page. Rainbows and shining suns are drawn on each side of these corner covers. Hannah recently told me that, when she looked at the diaries after our collaboration meetings, she remembered that Karen had made these and put them on each page when she had borrowed and read Hannah's diary and written this note. As Hannah said to me, "Isn't it amazing, she really is *in* the diaries!"

The note from Karen ends with an interesting comment, "keep smiling—you can always convince everyone you're happier than them!" This remark is striking on many levels. First, it gives yet another view of how others experience Hannah. Not only is she a robot, she is also always smiling, a quality I noticed years later when I met her. Yet, according to Karen, this smiling may be superficial. As she says, you can "convince" everyone, which seems to imply that Hannah's is an act. It may be experienced by others as being an act or at least Hannah's chum knows it is an act. Furthermore, this smile is experienced not only as artificial but also as competitive, as Hannah convinces everyone that she is "happier than them!" Yet, as her chum indicates, she is not so happy; she is just not expressing it to others.

On the other hand, this is where I am baffled. Just reading this letter, one would think Hannah was really struggling. Yet, nowhere in her entries is there a hint of despair or the need for consolation. Hannah, after all, is the peacemaker, she "sorts others out." As described in Chapter 1, these adolescent diaries initially put me to sleep, which was the first indication that Hannah's narrative was wrung tightly enough to absent important experience. This letter is the second indication that the diaries cover only a sliver of what is going on and that what is absent may be quite traumatic. [√√√]

Hannah's response to the letter is the most emotional reaction since her interactions with Tina:

- Felt like crying when I saw entry at back of diary. [Karen and her boyfriend] are such good friends, but almost too close to them now. Gone are the days of "happy" exteriors and now into adult life. Sounds awful at 16 but something has clicked of late!

That is stirring to read. It seems that she is experiencing a large shift in her experience of her self in relation to others. She is no longer able to present these "happy" exteriors regardless of her internal state, and she experiences this shift as being "awful." She is developing boundaries between inner and outer, and the interior that is being created is not so happy. She is not triangulating; no one is containing her discomfort. She is being forced to feel. So the fatiguing buoyancy of her text was a façade. Is this what has clicked? *[Hannah: responsibility, care, keep up the facade]*

The other stirring aspect of her response is her comment that although Karen and her boyfriend are "good friends," they are "almost too close now." While it is not clear what exactly being "too close" means, Hannah's response to this new-found awareness is quick and decisive. Indeed, after reading this letter, Hannah changes drastically. This letter and Hannah's response to it are an apex within the diaries. They stick up sharply, drawing attention to the lines, the words, the texture bubbling over, as the emotions threaten to burst the containment of the diaries. These emotions may be those previously contained by others within the group or those previously dissociated from her experience that Karen's safe chumship may have activated or threatened to pull into consciousness.

As Sullivan (1953) noted, chumships can be reparative. Perhaps the level of repairing needed for Hannah was too intense for her to handle within a chumship. All her difficulties around relating seem to be surfacing out of control. She is too close to Karen now. And what makes this apex so chilling is not only the content (after all, it is unclear what Hannah really means), but also that it marks the entry into a completely different way of living for Hannah. It marks the beginning of an isolating emotional desert. She activates her response, the very necessary response to this threat of being too close: to push the feelings out of awareness as violently as possible and to get away from the catalyst, Karen, her chum. Thus, in the following entries Hannah is on holiday, with no mention of the letter or Karen. When she returns, she suddenly leaves school, gets a job at a bank, and has little contact with her friends, including Karen. Instead, Hannah details her food, money, and shopping. She finalizes the stage she set earlier by dieting and exercising with Karen: for the development of anorexia and bulimia.

Davies and Frawley (1992, 1994) and Hegeman (1995) contend that dissociation is necessary for the other parts of the self to develop in a healthy or more functional manner. These diaries exemplify this statement. Hannah seems to face a choice of being possibly overwhelmed by whatever has "clicked" in her or reestablishing dissociation to save some parts of her self and continue functioning in the world. Interestingly, as mentioned previously about dissociating female bodies, it is the female body of chumship that must go. The need for Hannah to perform such a violent dissociation indicates just how powerful chumships can be, as Karen's intimacy not only helped Hannah develop into more than a robot, it also threatened her with disintegration.

Hannah stops writing of her chum; she literally changes the worlds in which she functions. In the past, if relationships in school became threatening, she created triangles to split friends and her affective responses away from her. But here, as she is beginning to create an exterior (implying that she may also be creating an interior), she is beginning to feel outside a triangle, which means she is experiencing differentiation with no capacity to control relational contact. Consequently, she may have little choice but to split herself off from Karen, the source of her feeling. But she does more than split off from Karen—she replaces her entire school environment with a significantly anonymous one: London. *[Hannah: didn't fit in—class, religion, language, maturity]*[6]

This decision to go to work is profound yet barely represented within the diaries. Hannah alludes to talking to Karen's father, a banker, about the business, but generally there is little sense of how or when this decision to leave school is made. It just happens. The relationship with Karen appears to be completely disrupted when Hannah goes to work instead of returning to school. Certainly work separates them physically as Hannah is no longer attending the same school, but it seems that Hannah recoiled after reading Karen's note. Gradually, she even stops writing of her in the diary except when she has penicillin poisoning. She says:

---

[6] Hannah said that she was middle class surrounded by upper-class girls at her school. She described being mature for her age, using adult language, and generally not fitting in with her peers. The only people to leave school that year were two poorly performing students who were into drugs, and Hannah, who was the top student in the class. So leaving school at 16 was extraordinarily odd. Yet it was not questioned by anyone, least of all her parents. She did leave ostensibly to work and to attend a college, which perhaps was seen as a step toward attending university.

- Phoned Karen to cheer me up. Didn't feel much happier but at least the problem was shared and she would cheer me up somehow.

Karen comes through:

- she too was ill and had bought me a bra, a beautiful purple comb and a snoopy book.

But when Karen calls weeks later and says, she "is feeling almost suicidal," Hannah writes no response in the diaries at all. According to the entries, she also does not call Karen the next day to cheer her up or to see how she is feeling. These omissions demonstrate just how distanced Hannah has become. In the past, such a call might have instigated a brigade of phone calls, but now it is barely a mention in the diary. *[Hannah: unable to hold other's pain as much?]*[7]

Two days later Hannah writes:

- Karen phoned and asked me where "my loyalties lay"? Can't think what she means.

Hannah does not discuss the conversation or how she responded. This entry is chilling to read because it is the moment I realize I have lost Hannah again. Absent in the beginning, she assumed the role of friendship cartographer. Then she appeared within the creation of her triangles and finally as an embodied person in relation to her chum. But here she disappears entirely. Her chum, in pain, is asking her where she is, and Hannah is so distanced and unreachable that she cannot understand the question. I see it as an indication of just how socially isolated she might be at this point. Not only is she at a loss to know the meaning of the question, she is also unaffected by it. She does not seem to care anymore that she and her chum no longer "understand" each other, they are no longer "similar." She is dissociated from any meaningful social contact, unable to comprehend the distress of her chum. [√√√]

At this point in the diaries, there is no real hint that Hannah has experienced any sexual or other trauma, except in her inabil-

---

[7] Hannah wrote "Hannah," referring to herself in the third person, regulating her painful self-experience while reading this analysis.

ity to relate and the gaping absences of experience in her narrative. However, it is significant that, having been sexually abused and physically invaded from an early age, Hannah had recoiled because of her relationship with Karen, the *body* of friendships. In childhood trauma, it is not only the memories of abuse but also the very experience of them, including the child's body experience at the time, that are dissociated (Davies and Frawley, 1992, 1994).

A competent adult self is constructed around "the screaming core of a wounded and abandoned child" (p. 16). This adult self is created by a child. The agendas of the adult and the dissociated child are radically different from each other. The adult seeks to forget, dissociate, hold her self together, while the child seeks a voice for the memories. These agendas work against each other. [√√√] *[Hannah: tough stuff]*[8]

There are no bodies in her diaries until she becomes friends with Karen. First, Hannah bonds with Karen through the attempts of both of them to get Karen's older brother to date Hannah, thus, creating a sexual body. Hannah uses Karen to focus all her sexual desire on her brother. Next Hannah's body emerges through food restriction and exercising. Last, Hannah's body emerges beside Karen's, in their underwear on the bed.

Although Karen and Hannah did not have an overtly sexual relationship, their friendship was extremely physically intimate and potentially sexually exciting. A function of chumship is negotiating homosexual desires within a heterosexist and homophobic culture. For Hannah to remain safe and functioning, she had to create not only relational distance, but also a particular neutered relational distance, emptied of any potential sexualization or embodiment. Her capacity to control all these forms of relational distance was profoundly compromised with Karen's physically intimate chumship. As such, it had to result in fragmentation, for Hannah's capacity to create this neutered relational distance was the only thing that stood between "Hannah the screaming child," and "Hannah the controlled adult." This response indicates just how effectively triangulation functioned to keep Hannah together. As a member of a dyad, Hannah could not control Karen's distance and she got "too close." Their intimacy

---

[8] Hannah found this theoretical model extremely helpful but also especially upsetting.

put Hannah in danger, and she may have had no choice but to recoil, to split herself off from the environment. [√√]

A Working Public Mind

On leaving school, Hannah develops an extraordinarily competent work self. In contrast to her indirect relational communications with friends, in the public business world Hannah is able to state her desires clearly and directly. When she goes to flea markets she takes great pride in being able to barter prices down. She lists the items she buys, notes the asking prices and the prices to which she bartered them, "got Kalari pot £1.50 for £1.00. One £26 for £23." When she is offered her first job in Windsor, she declines, saying she wants to work in London. She is then offered a position at a bank in London. After working three weeks she writes,

- Kim tried to get rid of all her nasty statements onto me but I got out of it. After all, I have been there 3 weeks now and I'm not just going to be stepped on.

Within the public world, Hannah demonstrates a keen sense of mobility and directness. She knows what she wants and takes it with no questions asked and no extraneous relations to be maneuvered. Hannah is savvy, direct, and quite successful in this world. Her success allows her to have relationships that actually support and reinforce a dissociated "adult persona" (Davies and Frawley, 1992, 1994). Her successful public interactions are the only relationships described in detail in the remainder of the adolescent diaries. [√√] *[Hannah: taught money at 6!]*[9]

One could also look at Hannah's ability to be clear and direct in the public realm as being similar to her peacemaking role with her friends. As a peacemaker, she solidified her alliances while rupturing those between others. This is a brilliant strategy for business (politics, war), where alliances must be protected at all costs, and it is better if one's connections jeopardize other people's positions. Relationally maneuvering or indirectly communicating is a complicated strategy that requires knowing where every competitor and coworker is and arranging matters

[9] Hannah said her father began teaching her basic accounting skills when she was six. These accounting lessons were the only nonovertly abusive activity she described as occurring with her father.

to get your way, ideally, with no one the wiser to your goals and desires. It is a perfect survival strategy for a business woman in particular, for she can be ambitious, powerful, and aggressive, operating under the radar, out of people's awareness.

Indeed, Hannah has a talent for the public realm that far exceeds her abilities interpersonally, and she is very successful in this world.

A Working Public Body

As described earlier, women survivors of sexual abuse succeed in the male public world not merely by dissociating the (female) child victim, but also by dissociating the (female) body. Hannah's female body peaked out within her chumship, but here it becomes bound and gagged by unyielding lists of money spent on items of food. These figures begin to take over the diary as Hannah records almost everything she eats for lunch and how much it costs.

- I went to Safeways and bought rolls and cheese, yoghurt and apple.
- It only cost 42p in comparison with MacD's which cost me 68p at lunch—and I've gone off it.

There is also a pattern in the food she chooses to buy to eat: a salad and baked apple; flan, a baked apple, and a glass of cold water; baked potato and apples; orange juice, a baked potato, and a greens and nut salad. Although she mentions having other foods at times, she either eats these most often or just repeatedly writes of them. The strangling repetition is a big red flag signaling possible trouble. In these last entries of her adolescence, I can virtually see Hannah caving into her self, pulling her skin tighter and tighter around her until it meets the bones. Here the narrative continuity that I identified as representing her self disappears and is replaced by a compulsive skeletal tally of money and food.

Once Hannah is alone in London, I realize how much I relied on her descriptions of other people's responses to her in order for me to hold on to her. There is a profound sense of anonymity that is more disturbing than the absence of her subjectivity earlier in the diaries. Once the social mirrors are gone, it seems that there is no longer an author. *[Hannah: sad reading]*[10]

---

[10] Hannah said this part of the analysis was the saddest for her to read, and it caused her to binge and purge once for the first time in years. It is

Nowhere in these adolescent diaries does Hannah's body appear with desire, appetites, or pleasure. Her body has been a site of struggle for control by others for friendships and by her minded self for diet and weight. Now her body appears on her terms, as an anorexic and bulimic object of her own control. But using eating disorders in this way means that, as she tightens her grip to create and find her self, she simultaneously slips through the cracks and disappears. This is the compelling, frustrating, and paradoxical nature of eating disorders. They function to resist the invasion of others and cultural ideals of feminine beauty by taking control of the expression of one's desires and one's body. But this control takes the form of self-destruction, molding the female body to both express and repress desire, objectifying it, and using it as a form of social currency, complying with the dictates of a misogynous culture.

These and other complexities of eating problems are explored in greater depth throughout the remainder of this book, focusing on her adult diaries. *[Hannah: fare dodge and some shoplifting commences here]*[11] *[✓✓]*

---

very important to note that it was the analysis of the adolescent diaries, with their remarkably *absent* traumas, and not the adult diaries, where the traumas begin to be named, that caused the most distress. For Hannah, the process of reading the analysis of her adolescent diaries was at least twotiered, including not only the experience of herself reading the content of the analysis but also her reexperiencing the absent traumas and filling in the "blanks" with her own embodied memories of abuse. This example demonstrates that there are multiple layers of conscious and unconscious relational experiences held and communicated within her diaries and this analysis.

11 She is able to slip through the cracks of society as well, by shoplifting and dodging underground fares. She really is invisible.

Chapter 5

Writing the Absented (Un)conscious in Hannah's Diaries

> I would embrace you and be embraced. But in this world, in this time, I must reach out to you in words. So day by day I render myself into words and pack the words into the page like sweets: like sweets for my daughter, for her birthday, for the day of her birth. Words out of my body, drops of myself, for her to unpack in her own time, to take in, to suck, to absorb.
>
> —J. M. Coetzee, *Age of Iron*

As I have described, absorbing Hannah's words from her diary/body was something that could not be done with ease, in my own time. It required losing my bearings and temporality and replacing them with Hannah's assaultive version. In this chapter, I impose my own timeline on her entries, which only gradually filled in the cracks of her childhood and adolescence with words. I hesitated to include this section for fear I would be giving away the plot, unfairly simplifying Hannah's life. Without such a plotline to begin to hang her entries on, however, it is quite impossible to understand what is going on from moment to moment. Her entries do not unfold in a way that the reader can build on to a life, probably because Hannah was not holding her experiences through time. Disturbances of time may signal psychic disturbances and these are often only in speech (Harris, 2005, p. 68) or, in this case, Hannah's writings. Hannah's adult diaries perfectly exemplify this observation.

In this chapter, I piece together a more digestible, somewhat linear life-narrative based on the stories in Hannah's adult diaries. These stories tell us about Hannah's childhood, the absented experiences from her adolescence, and her life between the end of the adolescent diaries and the beginning of the adult books. I also give away the action of the adult diaries by discussing her life as she was writing the diaries. The following three chapters then focus in greater depth on the primary relationship in these adult diaries—her marriage—and how she is able to transform herself and leave. This transformation, as it is represented in her text, brings to life the theory of temporal development outlined in Chapter 2.

Filling in the Absences

One of many things absented in the 1979 diary was that by the end, Hannah was spending most of her nights in her room bingeing and vomiting into a plastic bag to keep from alerting her mother, who was listening for the tell-tale multiple flushes of a purge. Such hypervigilantly invasive parenting was common in Hannah's house. Her parents literally treated her as a puppet, their hands in her body, their ideas filling her mind. *[Hannah: felt like a puppet with strings cut when mum died]* A typical story was her description of being given medicine when she was a young child. The scene, written as if it were stage directions for play, has her being pinned to the kitchen table, her parents tightly holding her arms and legs as they pried her mouth open, shoved medicine in, and then held her mouth shut until she swallowed.

As a child, Hannah suffered from eczema and asthma. Her mother became very involved tracking and controlling Hannah's bodily functions. She rubbed Hannah's skin with various ointments on "every part of [her] body," even continuing into Hannah's adolescence. When Hannah began menstruating, her mother demonstrated how to use tampons by inserting one into Hannah "with [her] legs apart." Hannah was not allowed to take a bath without her mother also being in the tub. Once she was married, her husband did the same. In fact, as the adult diaries begin, Hannah has not had a bath alone for the entire time of their marriage.

Both Hannah's parents force-fed her. Her mother, in a more common practice, did not let her leave the table until her plate was empty. Her father hated to eat and dreamed of having a "tablet meal." He regularly chewed and spat out his food at the table. If he overate, he would go to the bathroom and make himself vomit with a toothbrush and Hannah would clearly hear him retching. He not only controlled what and how much went into his body, he also controlled when things exited his body. He had a glass rod he would insert into his rectum to make himself move his bowels. He, in opposition to her mother, made Hannah leave food on her plate, but he coerced her to finish the food on *his* plate with threats that, if she did not, he would eat it and then be forced to make himself vomit.

Her father modeled multiple levels of disturbed eating. First, he was bulimic. He made himself vomit when he overate, and he purged by emptying his intestines with a glass rod. The introduction of this form of purging complicates things further; I cannot help but wonder whether this glass rod also functioned in a masturbatory way.

Next, he modeled dissociation and the projection of appetites, as he actively projected his disavowed appetite onto Hannah, making her finish his plate while leaving her own plate full. Third, he taught her not to eat out of her hunger or to trust her body. Not only did he not trust his body to tell him when, what, and how much to eat, he also did not trust it to expel properly either. Each major orifice needed to be controlled and regulated. Last, he created a confusing, disturbed, and chaotic environment within which to learn to regulate one's desires for food. As central as feeding is to the development of the capacity for temporal linking and going-on-being, Hannah's experience must have been fraught with confusion, tension, and frustration. While her mother's message seemed fairly direct and consistent (albeit invasive), her father's message was utterly confusing and abusive.

Her mother also controlled Hannah's contact with her father. She told Hannah that her father had never wanted to have children. She told her about his past relationships as if it were lurid gossip; they included an engagement and marriage to first wife who refused to have sex with him. Her mother also used Hannah as a substitute for her own body to sexually tease her father, who was extremely aloof. When Hannah got her first bra, her mother insisted that she "model" it for her father, so he would know he was "losing his little girl."

In response, her father would grab Hannah and pull her onto his lap to hold her there, in what felt to Hannah "a sexual way." He used Hannah to express his frustration with his wife. He complained to Hannah about his marriage and regularly threatened to leave the family. He constantly told Hannah of his unbridled disgust for his wife. In these ways both parents effectively erased Hannah in the service of triangularly communicating hostility to each other.

This sexualized contact with her father may have had even more impact because he was literally absent so much of the time. During our collaborative meetings, Hannah told me that as a child she used to read his date book to try to figure out who he was. Hannah said he had been a trained bomb defuser in world War II and had continued, after the war, to work for the Ministry of Defense. According to Hannah, his date book was written in code. His life was a mystery.

When her parents did communicate to her, as opposed to through her, the communication typically involved their teaming up to overpower her. In addition to administering medicines, neither would not allow her to have any morsel of her own experience. For instance, one time when they picked her up after a date they forcefully sat her between them and proceeded to interrogate and probe her until she told all about her sexual relationship. Once she did, her mother taunted her for days saying that she knew when Hannah slept with him as she could "see it in [her] eyes." Again her parents symbolically pinned her down and pried open her mouth to get at any experience Hannah may have had without them. Hannah cannot have her own body, behavior, emotions, or thoughts.

This level of invasion became surreal when, during our collaboration, Hannah said that her mother had claimed that she knew Hannah had had sex. She knew not only from Hannah's eyes, but also because she "smelled it" on her underwear. This disturbing comment indicates the profound level of invasion and lack of boundaries her mother exercised toward Hannah. It also highlights the sexualization of parental contact that Hannah must have experienced. Her mother did not literally touch her, but the shadow of sexual contact hung densely in the air (e.g., telling Hannah about her father's sex life) and behind closed doors (sniffing her underwear). Sexual abuse takes on a particularly creepy nature here because it exists under the skin, in the unacknowledged intentionality and unconscious of her mother. Sexual invasion becomes a way of being a woman, of being gendered, at the hands and mind of her mother's unconscious fantasies (Harris, 2005).

Similarly, Hannah's responses remain in these unconscious spaces in her adolescent diaries. The knowledge of her relationship with her mother adds an important layer to Hannah's relationship with Karen. Hannah may not have been able to differentiate between sexual, nurturing, and companionable intimacy (sexual contact always enlivens each of these), as they were all one forced invasion from her parents. While her relationship with Karen undoubtedly included its own sexual content, the experience of them both sitting on Karen's bed in their underwear must have felt like a wave of sexualized contact with no gradations of other forms of intimacy, and perhaps no sense of having control or effect on the level of this intimacy, including how she might desire to invade Karen.

Resisting Bodies

By animating Hannah's skin with their projected desires, her parents set the stage for Hannah to relate to her body as a foreign object to manipulate and speak through. Her body thus becomes the complicated site of her resistance. Hannah communicates many things through her body, including her need for distance within these oppressive relationships. In her family her distancing takes the form of bulimia, through which she uses her body as a wedge to separate from her mother. As she states, bulimia was "the first decision I took for myself and against mum." Her mother orders her to stop throwing up, and Hannah seemingly complies. She no longer vomits in the toilet when her mother is listening to the telltale flushes. Instead, she vomits into plastic bags in her room.

Given the level of invasive merging, Hannah's secret practices of embodied self-destruction are the only effective way of separating from her mother. Khan (1993) describes a secret as creating a space that can encapsulate and hold an absent self. So not only is the use of her body a site of destructive resistance, but also the physical use of her body creates a mental space, the capacity for some semblance of subjectivity in safekeeping. Her body can be used as a wedge creating a relational triangle of her self in secret safekeeping, her body, and her mother.

Bulimia, however, is not so simply analyzed here because her father was bulimic. While her mother controlled Hannah from the outside in, her father's control was from the inside out. He projected his appetite into Hannah by making her eat his food for him, where her mother created an appetite for Hannah separate from her own—"You must eat everything on your plate." Her father expanded his binge to include her body so she would do his bingeing for him and he did (her) his purging. As in a sexual penetration, her father's appetite and his food was forced down Hannah's throat. Given that the act of eating itself was one that diluted the boundaries between Hannah and her father, her bulimia is quite complicated. The process of bingeing and purging, together as a bulimic act, can hold her father in relation to her mother and maintain the family triangle. Hannah allies with her father behaviorally through bulimia as a secret against her mother. But the act of bingeing itself incorporates both her mother and her father, whereas the act of purging expels only her mother. Yet, by controlling the entire process of bingeing and purging, she takes over the one way in which they penetrated her. She resists and complies simultaneously.

In addition, outside this penetrating familial environment, Hannah was molested by a priest at school when she was about 10 years old. The priest led Hannah to the pool area and had her stroke his penis. Throughout our collaboration, Hannah mentioned this event as the primary sexual abuse of her childhood. It seems to me that, as horrible as this incident was, it was laid on a foundation of repeated physical invasions and sexual abuse from her parents. Even before the molestation, Hannah's sense of her self was being formed through her being pinned down having her orifices forced open and foreign bodies shoved in against her will. Here inner–outer and self–other melded into one uncontrollable and unregulated site of invasion.

Unfortunately, given the insidious repetition of abuse, Hannah's adult diaries recall tale after tale of sexual abuse by men. Describing her first sexual relationship, she says she "thinks [she] enjoyed sex" with him but she was "passive laying under him" and never touched him with her hands. She draws a picture disturbingly similar to that of her parents—she is pinned "under" him, hands immobile. She has an encounter with a man who "chats her up," and, even though she is scared, he is drunk, and they are in a train station, she follows him into an alley, as if caught in a tractor beam with no locomotion of her own. She does not mention what occurred.

When she is working in Germany, the company chairman "takes a liking" to her. He ritually abuses her by taking off her pants and asking her to tell him the English words for "vagina" and "clitoris" as he touches them and makes her stroke his penis. Then, during her marriage when she is on holiday alone in the United States, she "lets herself" get "abused" by various men while on a tour. Shortly afterward when she is in the hospital she "somehow ends up kissing another patient" ("It just happened"). *[Hannah: morn after pill]* Evidently, this incident may have involved intercourse, but, even at the time of our collaboration, Hannah was still uncertain what exactly had happened. She said that to "avoid any problems," the hospital staff had given her a morning-after pill. This way of sweeping the incident under the rug with no discussion probably reinforced the dissociation for Hannah surrounding this and similar sexual incidents.

Once she is separated from Eric, she has three sexual encounters; and, while she claims to enjoy them, she notes that she "could not say no" to them, and the first two in particular made her feel "disgusted" about herself. These incidents are thrown onto the pages with no exploration or detail, so that she seems to be walking through her life as a robot with her hands pinned down, unable to respond or reflect, even within the space of her own diaries.

The Story of Eric and Marrying the Invader

The story of Eric begins as Hannah's father lay dying from cancer. She brings Eric to meet her father the night before he dies, and he tells Eric to take good care of her. The sadistic torch is passed from one parent to the next, only this second abusive parent will be Hannah's husband. The night her father dies, Eric and she have sex for the first time. Eric, like her parents, controls Hannah physically, sexually, relationally, and psychologically.

In disturbing ways, Hannah's relationship with Eric mirrors that with her parents. It seems they both tied her up, but Eric ties her up for sex. They both invaded her "medically," but Eric puts cream on her bottom "with legs apart"; and both Eric and her parents punished her, Eric spanking her with a slipper. *[Hannah: abnormal labia]* Because Eric is in the medical field, his comments command a great deal of respect from Hannah, so that when he taunts her by telling her she has abnormally large genitalia, she believes him and feels quite grotesque. Eric, like her mother, has not let her take a bath alone for the entirety of their marriage. He tells her what to wear and how to keep her hair, nails, and makeup. He controls how much money she spends on clothes, even though she has her own quite lucrative job.

As the medical expert on her body, he controls Hannah's food intake and regularly weighs her. Like her parents, he controls the medications she takes. He also controls her sexually by coercing her to have sex when and where he wants. He makes her feel sick and abnormal for not having the same sexual desires. Controlling her social contacts, he isolates her by convincing her she does not need any friends. He controls her contact with her mother by not letting her visit or by refusing to stay at her mother's house for visits. He tells Hannah that her mother was "faking her illness when she said she had cancer and only had eight weeks to live," and again he refuses to let Hannah visit. After her mother died, he rushed Hannah to sell her mother's house, did not let her go thoroughly through her mother's things, and would not let her bring things from her mother's house into their house. He then put the money from the sale into a joint account, symbolically assimilating her mother.

Like her mother, Eric also tries to control Hannah psychologically by telling her he "knows all" her thoughts. He reorganizes her history by telling her that she was a "runt" and "unloved" by her parents, who "never wanted" her. He patronizes her by creating lists of chores for her to do and punishes her when she does not complete them. He "smacks her out" (hits her) when she almost had an accident driving on holiday and then punitively sends her off on her own to think about what she had done.

This control seems particularly insidious because it is exercised and maintained by Eric's continually making Hannah into the "sick child" and himself, in relation, into the omnipotent, medical parent. His control reenacts what Davies and Frawley (1992, 1994) describe as the dynamics between the abusive parent and the abused child. As Hannah writes, "My parents expected me to be complicit. [I] translated this dynamic to relationships with men." As Hannah struggles to "adjust to my new identity of marriage, changing my name and obedience to E. [Eric] instead of mum," she becomes whatever he wants from her and has "no separate identity" from him. Like her parents, Eric requires a surrender of boundaries and desires, but this surrender renders impossible love of both Eric and her mother simultaneously.

Somehow Hannah is stuck within yet another tumultuous triangle, this time of herself, her mother, and Eric. They are engaged in a "battle" in which Hannah is at the mercy of two "strong characters." The importance of this triangle becomes apparent when she says that, without her mother, Eric will be in charge. Without her mother to create space between Hannah and Eric, there will be no triangle, only a straight line leading Eric directly to her. So perhaps it is no surprise that, when her mother dies, leaving her with no relational buffer, Hannah fragments and is hospitalized.

The length of her inpatient hospitalization is not clear because the hospital had an open-admittance policy allowing her to come and go as she pleased. She usually had meals and slept there. She was there with no break for around a month, and then received day treatment for two more months. On weekdays she had multiple modalities of therapy, such as drama, art, individual, and group. During the weekends she usually went home to her husband. These entries signify a profound desperation. She often discusses suicide and is quite depressed. These diaries draw a picture of a woman who feels completely dependent on her husband for each move she makes and who, not surprisingly, feels profoundly helpless to change the course of her life.

Using her diaries, Hannah is eventually able to create a necessary triangle in her marriage to Eric. Unlike people in Hannah's life, the diary represents the one aspect of her life that Eric does not have access to. He cannot invade it, take it over or, threaten her out of. She continues to write in her diary even when she has to hide it or write when she locks herself in the bathroom at night. Her diary truly is the only "secret, private space" (Khan, 1993) that is not invaded by either her mother or Eric. And, while she complies with so many of Eric's demands, she continues her seemingly illicit relationship with the third member of this marriage, the diary. *[Hannah: only place of "noninvasion" like work in marriage]*

One could contest the use of Khan's secret space to describe Hannah's diaries. For Khan, the secret space freezes the self until it can be thawed out and animated as a subjectivity within a mutual relationship.[1] Writing and reading a diary is an interactive process that creates an intersubjective experience of the text's creating

[1] I thank Lawrence Jacobson for illuminating this point.

the reader and the reader's creating the text (Denzin, 1992). And the particular way Hannah played with the structure of her text created a process of improvisation by which she could collect representations of others and improvise relational interactions in order to create the capacity for experience and meaning making. As she said, "I didn't know who I was. I could see myself in the diaries, to work things out." She described her diaries as the only space where she was not invaded. Hannah's textual spaces may not be intersubjectively mutual in the strict sense of the word, but they are not an encapsulation of the self in suspended animation either. They represent a very important space between these capacities, where an invaded Hannah could begin to see herself and others, to become visible through a developmental process of creating temporal links that was exclusively and concretely under her control in her diaries.

All this said, perhaps it should come as no surprise that in the end, both Hannah and I would find out during the collaboration that her diaries actually had not in reality been so secret. Indeed, with uncanny timing, Hannah told me in our initial meeting that she had just seen Eric for the first time in years, after he called her out of the blue. When she told him about our research, he responded by telling her (and me) that he had already read her diaries and he knew everything they would tell me. In fact, he claimed that reading them during her last hospitalization was what had swayed him to get a divorce. So, not only did he continue to insert himself into her diaries and her current life by telling her she had no secrets, but he also penetrated our analysis, where her healing had led her. Like an explorer who "conquers" uncharted territory, he seemed to be saying that there was nothing that we could know that he did not already know.

Of course, this incident was most likely a response to finding out that someone was reading and also analyzing and planning to publish the stories leading up to their divorce. As he evidently knew, he did not come off very well in her diaries. Given his own needs for control, this realization must have upset him. And, true to form, he responded by penetrating Hannah in the moment confessing a past invasion of her diaries. He told her he already knew what the diaries contained and blamed them, the Hannah-created third in their relationship, for his having asked for a divorce. One might also ask, although in the moment I did not, why Hannah met with him then, just before our collaboration meeting? And, knowing him as she did, why did she tell him about it? To gain his permission? Guilt? Did he know what was going on unconsciously? This event ended up creating a prismatic triangle of myself, Hannah, and Eric all connecting through her diaries.

This new-found knowledge may shift how this analysis of her adult diaries is read. I did not include it in the exploration of her adult diaries because I cannot be certain he actually did read them and becuase Hannah wrote them and interacted with them in the moment as if they were indeed her secret. It is Hannah's creation of these diaries and the stories they contain that is the focus of this book.

Throughout the first 10 diaries, Hannah is piecing together the past and struggling to assess her relationship with Eric. In the process, she begins to play with the structure of her text by using diagrams, lists, and plays to contain her experiences. As she does so, her chaotic stories of abuse and self-destruction are gradually folded into a past, present, and future. Stories and people begin to have definition and bounded outlines. Then, and only then, Hannah emerges as a subject who is not merely a vessel for others' desires and intentions. Interestingly, in the 11th diary, as she is heading toward a divorce and emerging within her text with a distinct, skinned boundary, she begins writing in a hard-cover book. But these are not simple decisions, for she also attempts to overdose three times. Throughout this narrative sequence of contemplated separations followed by overdoses, she seems to awaken progressively. Once they separate, she starts her own very successful human resources consulting business and travels alone for business all over the United Kingdom and Europe.

The last diary, which comprises only lists, brings together a collection of the people in her life like the credits rolling at the end of a movie. Here all the characters and their respective pasts are presented as she explores how each person has helped construct and influence her development and how she thinks she would like to continue her growth.

Throughout these adult diaries it is her shifts from prose to lists, to diagrams to plays, to prose again, that provide a needed structure to her story. It is in the structure that it becomes apparent that Hannah and her diaries function as one body. As such, the diaries create a capacity accumulating her experiences in unique ways. Because Hannah is not able to accumulate and integrate these recreations internally, she collects them within her text in two distinct ways, in the content and structure of the text, each holding different aspects of her experience. These spaces of content and structure are so split from each other in the diaries that I have distinguished them here and in the following chapters as well.

The guiding structure of this analysis of her adult diaries is her evolving capacities for differentiation and temporal linking. I focus first on the ways in which she attempts to resist or comply with Eric toward her own differentiation (Chapter 6) and then on the ways in which she attempts to regulate her newly emerging self (Chapter 7). Mirroring this complex process, the structure of her text evolves and shifts (Chapter 8). The developmental trajectory described in Chapter 2 comes alive in these last three chapters through examples provided from Hannah's diaries.

Chapter 6

Resisting to Differentiate / Differentiating to Resist

Resistance is a complicated word. In psychoanalysis it is usually pejorative, as "the name given to motivational forces operating against growth or change and in the direction of maintenance of the status quo" (Ghent, 1990, p. 110). In feminist theory it involves liberation. Resistance is bound by context to the psychological and social structures that are being resisted (Hoy, 2004), and not all forms of resistance are readily identified as such.

Shifting focus from the individual to the cultural body similarly affects how we explore eating disorders. Viewed clinically, they are self-destructive and often resistant to treatment. At the same time, eating disorders are a defiant thorn in the cultural body's side. Through them, women resist the traditional female gender role. Women become too thin to reproduce, too fat to fit into the feminine ideal of beauty, too controlling and distant to penetrate fully. If the social order relies on the capacity to split off and contain female bodies, then, women's taking any kind of control over their bodies (whether eating because of one's hunger; sleeping when one is tired; deciding when, if, where, and with whom one will have sex; or bingeing and purging, starving, and cutting oneself) is a form of defiant resistance. But this defiance not only functions to resist external forms of control, it also creates an experience of a skinned body with a coherent temporality, which can help counter the impact of trauma. Bingeing and purging or waging a hunger strike (Orbach, 1986) can create feelings of control in a powerless situation and allow a woman to resist frightening and overwhelming memories and experiences (Schwartz and Gay, 1993).

Yet by locating the struggle in the body, women with eating disorders are accepting and enacting the cultural mandate to sacrifice the (female) body for the safety of the (male) psyche. In so doing, they deny their own sense of, and entitlement to, their embodied appetites and subjectivities. They use the female body as currency as clearly and destructively as does the culture.

Thus, resistance is a complex process, for it functions simultaneously as both traumatic and subversive repetition. Which version of resistance appears to be central depends on our focus. Resistance can be conscious and unconscious, self-destructive and growth promoting. Most important, it may be only through an act of resistance that we are able to know what it is we need to resist. Even when it appears to be complicity, resistance can open new possibilities for being (Hoy, 2004).

As the second part of Hannah's story begins, she binges and purges regularly and uncontrollably, shoplifts, and compulsively masturbates. She fears going shopping and is generally unable to do daily tasks such as remembering her way home in the car. She is entirely dependent on Eric to move within the world. The adolescent peacemaker is gone; yet, seamlessly continuing from the end of the 1979 diary where we left off, she goes on to detail her food. These details of food, and now weight, are the only continuities in these adult diaries. They are not just areas of control for her. Through her eating disorder, she creates her own isolated, skinned body, albeit one that has limited capacities for psychological growth. Her detailed entries of food and weight are the only spaces where her own intentionality and resistance peek out from underneath her smothering, abusive relationship with Eric.

It should be no surprise, given the previous discussions of female development, that young women aged 16–24 are particularly vulnerable to abusive relationships (Raghavan et al., 2005). Just when males are expected to compete, fight, take up their privileged space in the public realm, females are expected to recede, hide their competences, bury their aggression, shrink their expanding bodies, and live through the desires of others (Gilligan, Lyons, and Hanmer, 1990; Gilligan, Rogers, and Tolman, 1991; Brown and Gilligan, 1992). The paradoxical functions of eating disorders can work well to help navigate these oppressive expectations and the abusive relationships to self and others that develop from them. For Hannah, all her competence, intelligence, and creativity are squeezed into this one limited, resistant–compliant area of her life. Her eating disorder becomes as central to her survival in her abusive marriage as it is to her destruction.

This chapter focuses on Hannah's first five adult diaries. As described earlier, in these diaries, Hannah exists solely in relationships. The relationship itself creates the skin within which she lives, and without it she ceases to exist. There are no boundaries of time in these diaries. All her previous abusive relationships are current and ongoing within her present relationships, such that just reading her narrative leaves one uncertain which events are past or present. Experience here is decidedly not "embraced by time" (Loewald, 1980); Hannah has no capacity to create temporal links, no way to make meaning of her experiences, no way to self-regulate. The developmental house of cards described in Chapter 2 as the creation of time and space has not even begun to be built by Hannah at this point. Her access to secondary process—symbolization, which emerges only with the capacity to create temporal links—is extremely limited.

Reading this untimed narrative with its handicapped symbolic organization creates a multilayered effect. The story is chaotic and difficult to follow, but a coherent story emerges as we watch Hannah walk through her life with no intentionality of her own. In this story, we can see that it is not just that Hannah needs a merged "other" in order to evacuate her overwhelming and confusing experiences, she does not even know how to create these experiences. As she was with her parents, Hannah and Eric function as one body, within one inflexible skin.

Hannah and Eric have been married for nine years. Her mother and father have both died from cancer. Eric is her only family and, because he thinks she does not need friends, she does not have any. While her adolescent diaries focus exclusively on her public life, these focus exclusively on her private life with Eric.

In this chapter, I outline the ways in which Eric seems to contain, control, and dictate to Hannah by "keeping" her desires, her image, and her affective experiences. But as the chapter unfolds, it becomes quite murky as to who is dictating this "keeping," and which repetitions are traumatic and which are subversive.

Eric as the Keeper of Hannah's Desire

- On the road again from 1.30 to 4.30 and then a quick tea stop. Had a cup of tea and again E. said 'I think you should have something to eat" had a slice of hazelnut cake. I know he means well, but I can't always bring myself to take a piece initially.
- I had salad as second [course]. Shared with E. and his choice. I really wanted pasta. Didn't eat much salad; said too cold for it. Couldn't eat all meal. E. ate small and I couldn't eat any more than him.
- Out for dinner after tears of talking. E. and I both chose chicken salad; I ate half. Felt trapped and tearful—wanted to run out as full and knew had to eat desert and cheese. As tearful E. said could have drink and no food. Still sad. On way home wanted to vomit, felt sick and wanted to feel happy feeling after sickness. E. wanted me to eat tea and choc biscuits. [I] Said he'd said I didn't have to eat. He said [that] was only in restaurant. Felt trapped again.
- Towards end of meal E. said "I didn't have to eat all' so I left rest. Just what my Dad said. Towards end had enough savory was interested in a desert and E. said 'are you sure. I'm very full. You're not on a binge are you?'. [E's comment] meant I couldn't eat.
- When I'd gone to the restaurant. I chose asparagus salad, boiled chicken'; beans; peas; ratatouille. He said 'gosh you've got a lot on your plate—don't eat it all if you can't' He refused a bread roll so hard for me to eat.

In these entries Eric clearly acts as the keeper of Hannah's desires. He tells her what and how much to eat. He chooses food at restaurants and usually makes them share entrées. When

Hannah eats more than he thinks she should, he asks, "Are you sure? You're not on a binge are you?"—which stops Hannah in her tracks. When she does not eat as much as he thinks she should, he forces her to eat. When they are at a restaurant Hannah ends up in tears because Eric will not let her leave until she has finished her dessert. And when they return to their hotel room he changes the rules and forces her to eat more. Eric dictates her hunger in confusing and unpredictable ways. He makes her eat one night, stops her from eating the next, then accuses her of bingeing when a hint of her own desire creeps in. She feels trapped, and, indeed, like a caged animal, she is unable to control not only her eating but also her access to food.

This holding or dictating her hunger recreates the relationship Hannah had with her father around food. As described, he simultaneously told her to eat lightly and leave the food on her plate, while blackmailing her into finishing all the food on his plate. Eric easily fills her father's shoes. Hannah can never eat more than he does even if he is not hungry and she is. Her body ceases to exist, and they live only through his; they are enveloped by one controlling, tightly wrapped, "limiting membrane" (Winnicott, 1971). In this body she does not have to hold or even experience any desires around food, her hunger, or satiation, for he does it for her. There is no space between, no need for the capacity for temporal linking. Like that of a conjoined twin, Eric's body processes and creates all experiences. This is not an entirely bad deal. Eric can grant Hannah permission to eat. When they stop for tea, she is not able to ask for a piece of cake until Eric says she should eat one. She says, "I know he means well, but I can't always bring myself to take a piece initially." There is relief in not having to make the decisions that come with the creation of experience.

Having been raised by two parents who made no room (literal space) for the development of her own recognition of (let alone regulation of) her appetites, she needs Eric's capacity for. He minds her temporal linking for her. He creates her experience. Consequently, she never learns to differentiate her appetites, and she does not have to take responsibility for eating. This process of externalizing her appetites perfectly supports her bulimic endeavor, as, continuing to dissociate her experiences of her appetites and her body, she allows Eric to dictate and control them. She just has to follow Eric's rule that they exist as one body.

Erasing Hannah's Desires for Sex

- Had sex and can accept and don't need to come.
- Had sex by sucking E. and then settled to go to sleep.
- Feel sick again today. Had sex last night and didn't really enjoy.
- Worried about the sex. The thing is I find it hard to say no. Ironically the first thing I did last night was give him sex—yet I don't want, enjoy, or like myself for it. Today feel depressed and ate cake and vomited. A pattern?

Given Eric's role of keeping Hannah's appetite for food, it is no surprise that he also keeps her appetite for sex. Those diary entries typify how Hannah describes sex in her diaries. Brief snippets such as those are plopped at the end of an entry, unlinked and disconnected from the rest of the content. Not surprisingly, given this dissociated presentation, there is also no written subject of the action. Unlike eating, where it appears clear that Eric is in the lead, with sex, it is unclear who is initiating which activity or what exactly is happening. Does she want to have sex? Does Eric want to have sex? What is sex? Is it oral sex? Intercourse? Is there a difference? Who decides what kind of sex to have? Is she being forced, coerced? Is it as it is with food and she needs him to give her permission? Among all these questions, I have only one certainty: she does not write of enjoyment or pleasure. In fact, the only time she writes of a subject of the action is when she uses the pronoun "I" as she is describing not wanting to have sex, not being able to say "no," not enjoying it. Given this observation, Hannah does write of desire in the diaries, only it is a desire not to have sex.

As the diaries progress, Hannah's desire appears less in the negative as she writes:

- Had sex but I didn't have an orgasm. Need more time for me and sad it's not made all the time.

Here it becomes apparent that, like food, sex, too, involves only one body and one orgasm—Eric's. But while Hannah's appetites for food are inextricable from Eric's, with sex, Hannah appears to be able to create some separation. She knows she needs more time. Indeed, she seems to have a notion that she, too, should have an orgasm. So perhaps her desires for sex are not so much in the negative—it is not that she does not want to have sex, she does not want to have what constitutes sex in their relationship, that is, an activity that results in Eric's orgasm only.

- Worried about sex and affection. Will tell E. at a nonsensitive time about fears of being rejected if initiate sex. Also will say am going to discuss sex topic in FT on Monday so he is warned.

When Hannah considers discussing sex with Eric, she plans to do it during one of their family (couples) therapy sessions. This discussion requires preparation, which involves "warning" Eric ahead of time. But this warning must be done at a "nonsensitive" time. She must mold her fears, desires, and needs around his moods and sensitivities. It is fatiguing just to read how much controlled, careful planning is required for Hannah to position herself relationally to discuss sex "properly." All this work, and she does not even get to have an orgasm.

- Got to talking about sex I said I have no feelings of desire but ok when started. He said I should do it for him. I asked how often he'd like sex and he said 5 times a week. I feel that's ~~excessive~~ unreasonable when I'd choose nil. We agreed to start with 3 times a week—maybe 1x intercourse, 2x oral sex and start with. I put in cap when I want. If either of us definitely don't want sex we should say when we get into bed so other knows and we can go straight to sleep.

When they do finally discuss sex, it is a business negotiation in which Hannah is working hard to hold her ground. They plan the amount and the type of sex they will have. She will give him oral sex twice a week and then have intercourse once a week. The deal is set, and neither partner was distracted by desire during the negotiation. But there is still no orgasm for Hannah.

At this point in the analysis of Hannah's diaries, I find it is impossible not to feel a parallel process of frustration, control, invasion, and desire. Reading entry after entry of Hannah's not wanting sex, robotically having it anyways, saying it is OK, then saying it is not; not wanting to eat, eating anyway, feeling fat, feeling relieved Eric made her eat—I get frustrated. What does she want? I am reminded of Meg's comment from the adolescent diaries, that the group did not trust Hannah because they did not know where she stood. Similarly, I wonder where she is, what her passion is. Oddly, as much as I hate Eric's control and sadism, I find myself identifying with him and wondering what it is like to live with Hannah. Is his sadistic control released because of frustration or an inability to please Hannah? Or does he not even notice?

I remember the difficulties I had negotiating the collaboration with Hannah and how, denying the boundaries she craved, she initially agreed to everything. I remember how she took extra work for the week of our collaboration meetings, which made me feel like a burden, having to fit into her much more important schedule; how she later described it as her response to her fears that I would not spend enough time with her. I want to be able to differentiate my actions with Hannah, and my responses to her text, from Eric's abuse, but it is difficult for they are not so clearcut. Sure, unlike Eric, I did not tie her up and invade her, but, then, I did not have to. She willingly complied. What a powerful relational position it is to live with no desires, no way to be pleased.

Hers is invisible but potent resistance. It is profoundly disruptive to the system (e.g., my collaboration schedule and Eric's invasions of her body); and, while it is not effective at lessening Eric's control over her, it does seem to shift the way she relates to his control. As these diaries proceed, Eric's hold on Hannah's desire appears to crack further when she details what is clearly her own sexual desire.

- I feel abused by so many men that even with E. I sometimes feel guilty. Maybe when in my fantasies it is either forced or not me i.e. another role

> or times gone by. Maybe only then can I accept myself in sex" [She fantasizes about being forced to have sex and/or she dissociates and imagines someone else is having sex].
> Find I need fantasies to enjoy sex.
> sexuality w/E—can cuddle/kiss
> —not interest in sex
> abuse issues—sexual turn on
> —still sexual interest
> —satisfy myself

We see her struggling here, not necessarily to identify her desires, but to allow herself to hold them. As she writes, "maybe" her fantasies involve forced sex, "maybe" she needs fantasies to accept her desire. This tentative voice becomes strong when she shifts to a list. The importance of lists is discussed in detail in Chapter 8, but suffice to say that the structure of lists provides a tighter limiting membrane than does prose. Here she clearly states three different times that her sexual desire is linked to her fantasies, not to Eric, and that these fantasies are often recreations of abuse. These recreations indicate that time and space are abundant here, as Hannah is experiencing sex in multiple times and places at once. She may be having sex with Eric in the present, but, recreating various situations of her past abuse, she is also fantasizing about being forced and overpowered by someone, or she imagines she is watching someone else having sex. Sexual fantasies like these serve many different functions for Hannah.

Although she may feel she deserves an orgasm, Hannah cannot allow herself to hold her sexual desire. Fantasies about being overpowered allow her to enjoy sex by placing her guilt or disturbing feelings about sex in the fantasized situation and not in her physical response. This way, it is not her body that is betraying her, but the other person. This other person exists only in fantasy and thus is under her control this time. These different fantasies also allow Hannah to split her emerging sexual desire into different scripts, times, and places, ensuring nothing overpowers her. She can buffer one desire with another, a made-up fantasy with reality. These different fantasies enable Hannah to act out different roles.

As noted earlier, Davies and Frawley (1992, 1994) have written about the various configurations of relational desire that allow a survivor to play the abuser, victim, or rescuer in an attempt at integration. Similarly, Freud (1919) described the masochist being beaten as simultaneously identifying with and fantasizing that she is the sadist doing the beating. Meanwhile, the sadist is fantasizing that he is the masochist being beaten.

In her fantasies, Hannah can play the roles of masochist/victim, sadist/abuser, rescuer/witness. She can enjoy sex in one scenario, be disturbed by it, and create a different dyad having sex in another; she can absent her body altogether and just watch the action; or she can struggle to integrate the past in a recreation. Through all these fantasies, she avoids having sex with Eric in the moment. She can keep herself from being temporally pinned down by being in a number of different times simultaneously. The problem is that wherever she is in the fantasy, she is still allowing herself physically to have sex with Eric although she does not want to. She is still being pinned down in space, even as she is escaping in time.

This analysis illustrates that the very act of creating an embodied experience is probably traumatic for Hannah, for it necessarily entails connecting with her experiences of abuse. Her fantasies are potentially retraumatizing because of their violent content, but they may create a space for her to claim some desire. She does have desire, and in some ways she clearly knows her desire, but she does not speak it or place it within a relational space. It is projected onto Eric one moment, contained in lists the next, spoken in the negative when she desires not to have sex with Eric, and then it is seen peeking out from behind a memory of abuse that she describes as being sexually exciting. Desire is a hot potato that must be thrown into another. In doing so, Hannah, in relation to Eric, retains the power of having no desire. She does not need another body for an orgasm. She can evacuate all her desires and watch them work on Eric and make him want to control her. She can emerge the victor in this sexual negotiation, while remaining his captive in their marriage.

Recall that in the chapters exploring her adolescent diaries, she learned how to refract her desires and get around the cultural dictates abnegating female desire. Having Meg tell the other girls when it was Hannah's birthday was a training incident for her marriage, in which she can be only the subject of her desire to appear to be an object in relation to Eric. So her subjectivity is quite slippery. She is there and not there simultaneously. Because she must constantly project her desires onto others, her only form of temporal linking casts these desires as emanating not from within, but as an invasion from the outside. Consequently, her projected desires and Eric's desires are probably indistinguishable, leaving her feeling as a powerless object of his whims.

Eric as the Keeper of Hannah's Image and Experience

- Went to bed and he saw my nails—hand and toes—I'd cut them very low in anger one evening. I said it's cos I don't like myself and don't care about my appearance. He was quite angry and said if not for me I should make an effort for him

    E's view was I need to pull myself together—eat normally, put on makeup daily and especially when I get home, [wear] sexy clothes and no knickers sometimes to feel sexy not worry if I get fatter—just do it for his sake if not mine and maybe I'll enjoy it. Also grow my nails and take time for myself. He suggested writing a list of positive action points carrying round with me pinning on fridge etc. and agreeing to do. I'm not sure if this is me—feels like what I'm being told to do. I suppose I can give it a try. Trouble is it's back to acting and not sorting out underlying problems.

Yet another struggle for control of Hannah's body revolves around her appearance and image. In that example, Eric sees that Hannah has cut her nails off and is scratching her legs and making marks on them. Eric buckles down and jumps further into her to control every crevice of her experience. He details the image he wants her to project, if only for him. This is literally an image; it is not about Hannah's finding or creating her self, or even deciding what image she wants to convey.

It is Eric's wish that she come home from work and stay dressed up all evening, keep her hair down, her makeup and jewelry on, and have perfectly painted nails. But he moves beyond the image by stating that she should also be in a good mood for him in the evenings. He tells her how many times each week he wants to have sex, and he insists that they construct a list of ways she should keep up her appearance. And, if penetrating her body and mind here is not enough, he suggests that they write this list in her diaries and then post it on the refrigerator so that they can both be reminded of her goals.

Here Eric tells Hannah to put her body, literally and symbolically, on display for him. He wants her to be an object without any desire (she should just have sex for him) or needs of her own (she should keep herself attractive to and for him). But he is also penetrating her symbolic body—her use of lists in her diaries. He becomes a focus of one of her lists, and she will have to rip it out of her diary, her only safe and private space, to hang it up. He will jump inside her private space, create a foreign body, make her rip it out of herself, and then place it on public display. As is elaborated in the next chapter, Hannah's diaries and her lists create a "third" in their relationship and provide some semblance of relational buffer for Hannah. These diaries and lists also serve a therapeutic function for Hannah. Therefore, Eric's penetrating them is yet another violent act of domination. She was a puppet annexed by her parents, and now Eric is attempting to inhabit her entirely.

Ironically, by creating the Hannah he expects, as opposed to the Hannah that exists, Eric is not getting closer to Hannah. Instead, he creates another third in their relationship. Placing this idealized body on the refrigerator creates space between the real Hannah and himself. Like repetitions, Eric's action creates both further trauma and the potential for subversion.

First, Eric's action is an additional, insidious invasion of Hannah that succeeds in further splitting her psyche and soma. Again, when a caretaker is not attuned to the infant, development proceeds only by splitting the psyche and soma, with the psyche dominating the desires of the soma (Winnicott, 1958a, 1970).

Here Eric is taking advantage of this split, which was created by years of abuse. Entering and traveling freely within this space, he further splits them apart by creating an objectified, idealized version of Hannah. His role as the one who knows how often to have sex, how much she should eat, what she should look like, solidifies his position within this triangle, fueling her already potent distrust of her body and enhancing her dependence on him as the expert psyche. As such, Eric provides the space for Hannah to remain bulimic. He stands in the way of her recovery, not only with his openly sadistic control of her appetites and appearance, but also because their relationship is based on a triangulated way of relating that necessitates a huge split between Hannah's mind and her body. She cannot trust her body and remain with Eric because he cannot tolerate her having her sense of her own body and her own relationship with her body. He has to remain a translator, intercepting and distorting communications. She must remain sick in order to remain married to Eric.

By fueling her distrust of her body, Eric sides with the abusive parent persona (Davies and Frawley, 1992, 1994) that Hannah has internalized. By supporting her identification with the aggressor (her parent), he reinforces that she deserved to be abused. Hence, her body—the container of her memories of trauma and abuse—must be innately bad. She cannot possibly rely on it for any form of knowing, and she must continue to dissociate it and its contents. By reinforcing the strength of her internalized abusive parent, Eric validates her notion that she cannot trust her memories or her body. There is no possibility for Hannah to integrate her psyche and soma or to be able to experience herself as being real. And living in and of the world as a dissociated being means that she has no internal compass, no sense of who she is, what she wants, what she is really experiencing. She must continue to look to Eric to tell her all about herself, thereby solidifying the circle of her abuse.

But creating the ideal Hannah also helps Hannah. As Davies and Frawley contend, healing from trauma requires that the adult persona acknowledge both the dissociated embodied memories of the abused child and the part of herself that allied with the abusive parent to blame herself for the abuse. With Eric standing as the gatekeeper between her body and her mind, she does not have to tackle this frightening and potentially fragmenting rapprochment. She is not threatened with integration. The importance of this function cannot be overemphasized.

Existing without agency (the capacity for temporal linking) is like walking through a world of chaos with no sense of where to begin, what direction to take, what is up, down, or sideways. Self-destructive violence can link internal intentional states with external events (Fonagy and Target, 1998). This violence can create the skin, the limiting membrane differentiating inner from outer, self from other, and enable the emergence of spatial orientation. Cutting, bingeing and purging, and other forms of self-destruction also become a concrete, physical representation of cause and effect, of time. But because this time-and-space, this temporal linking operates literally on the skin, or in the food taken in and expelled, it does not require the creation of an internal space, a capacity for.[1]

As we will see in the next chapter, each time Hannah is suddenly faced with integration, she attempts to overdose, reinscribing self-destructive violence as temporal linking. Here, as Eric becomes aware of her growing attempts at self-mutilation (which are occurring as she is beginning to speak about sex in family therapy), he reinserts himself as the keeper of her desires. While this reinsertion does keep Hannah from creating her own links, it also saves her from further self-destructive violence. Eric is saving her from having to experience her self prematurely, before she has developed her own capacity for temporal linking.

Second, by creating an ideal Hannah, Eric has inadvertently created a larger space for Hannah's resistance. With each decree he hands down, Hannah creates a secret space (Khan, 1993) within which to encapsulate her self in hiding. Through her secrets, she creates a space to begin to hold herself. So when Eric tells her to stop writing in her diary, she hides it and writes in the middle of the night while she has locked herself in the bathroom.

---

[1] Fonagy and Target (1998) seem to assume the presence of internal intentions, which implies the existence of an internal space. For Hannah, I wonder if she has had the opportunity to create such an internal space. Even when such a space does exist, the use of self-destructive violence indicates that this space has been dissociated and is inaccessible for the creation of temporal linking. The process then is transferred to the skin or into other physically self-destructive behaviors where linking becomes concrete and visible.

When he tells her to keep up her appearance for him, she undermines this control by noting that he is asking her to act, not to "sort things out" more deeply. She uses Eric's order to differentiate between "manufacturing the feelings of being a genuine person" (Guntrip, 1971, p. 149) and working toward being able to be one. With each attempt at control, Eric seems to create the space for Hannah's differentiation. This aspect of resistance is flushed out more fully in the next chapter.

Eric as the Keeper of Affective Experience, or Hannah Using Eric as a Container?

I have alluded to the possibility that, as controlling as Eric is, Hannah may participate in this control by using Eric to contain her experiences. This complex process requires a more in-depth look, which is provided by focusing on one of the rare family therapy sessions when Hannah gets angry. As she writes:

- E. was asked his greatest fear. Was that if he was critical, I would leave him. That he is being tested—if he doesn't agree to address problem areas (e.g. anger, and sex) I will leave him. I replied they are problems and part of why I'm in therapy. He was very literal—"You came into therapy due to your mum not our marriage." Explained slowly—in mental shorthand and less literal then E. [I] Said I did come in and addressed childhood/eating issues but feel there is dysfunction in sex life and anger and I cope through inappropriate images [fantasies] and food. Want to give up old ways and have healthy new ones. E. was very scared of my response even though I'd heard his fear before.

  Lili explained he had choices too. I wasn't one with all power—he could say what he wanted too. Then L. asked what I feared, round anger—E.'s at me; my hurt of him as "child," my "failure" of him as a mother and repeat of his mother leaving him after he had trusted her. As he pushed a little about anger, I was tearful and my mind became chaotic—I couldn't think logically anymore—just cried. E. said [I] couldn't say anything yet as I'm too vulnerable—clearly I am and L. talking very slowly. E. also explained we don't get angry—I've taught him to speak "personnel" speak and we both intellectualize issues. Don't ever express true anger—indirect; patterns around each other; snap at each other etc.

In this entry, Hannah becomes angry at Eric for saying he thinks if "he doesn't agree to address problem areas" she will "leave him." She describes having to use "mental shorthand" for Eric to understand her thoughts. Eric becomes "scared." Lili, the family therapist, then asks Hannah what she fears around anger, and Hannah responds that she fears hurting Eric. Eric "pushed" her about her anger and she immediately decompensates within the entry: "I was tearful and my mind became chaotic—I couldn't think logically anymore." And as she is decompensating, Eric steps in to protect her from Lili. He says she is "too vulnerable" to continue and explains that as a couple, "We don't get angry."

This interaction seems to demonstrate the dynamic of Hannah's taking the role of the sick child as if to make herself impotent in relation to Eric's power. But by doing this, she does not have to experience her anger; indeed, she is not allowed to experience her anger. Instead, she decompensates, and Eric takes care of her by ending the inquiry. He gains control through Hannah's losing her voice and becoming mentally chaotic. And, in her chaos, Eric emerges as the rational, logical one who knows about their interaction patterns. He can be the one to tell Lili how things are in their marriage, because Hannah is too sick to continue, even though, only two lines before, Hannah was the one using "mental shorthand" to try to explain something he was unable to understand.

That is only one example of many in which Hannah seems to defer power to Eric by becoming a sick, helpless, vulnerable child to his omnipotent parent. As she hints during the family therapy session, her anger is so powerful she can hurt Eric. Indeed, turned inward, it causes her to decompensate. Harris (1997) contends that, more than anything, women fear hurting others with their anger, and, as described in Chapters 3 and 4, they often do not have the opportunities to develop the capacities to create temporal links to help self-regulate and symbolically express their anger. In that case, Hannah's anger might be so powerful that she is too frightened to hold on to it even within the family therapy environment. It is easier to be a sick child in relation to a powerful parent than to be an angry woman in relation to a weak man.

Therefore, she may fear Eric's dependence, vulnerability, or any sign of weakness. He must be strong and in control.

Here she is not only decompensating under the weight of her anger, she is desperately attempting to cover Eric's sudden vulnerability, apparent when Hannah must use "mental shorthand" with him. Here the restrictions on gender limit Hannah to either/or experiencing. Either she is strong and he is weak, or she is weak and he is strong. There is no way to share power or to empower one another. It is a dog-eat-dog relationship, and Hannah knows to let Eric emerge as the strong man and he knows how to help her emerge as the weak woman.

This line-by-line analysis indicates that the dynamic of power in their relationship is not clear cut. Certainly Eric is abusive, and he has a great deal of power in their relationship. Hannah has to use "mental shorthand," however, to explain things to Eric. She fears the power of her anger to hurt Eric. Her power and his vulnerability work together to keep her a passive victim.

Who Leads in This Sadomasochistic Dance?

- E. scared [on ski run] and I felt guilty not looking after. He says he's my first child.
- Arrived in village for the night after I drove last 25 km. Once drove off edge of tarmac by lay-by and E. grabbed wheel. Very dangerous and I [was] smacked out [hit by him]. He said he was just about to say I'd been doing so well. Of course, [he] never did say. I was 'sent off' for 1 1/2 hrs on own. Felt I'd not done well.

These entries exemplify the paradox: Hannah is at once the weak, misbehaving child in need of a "smacking out," and the powerful parent of Eric, her "first child." So who is leading in their sadistic–masochistic dance? To address this question, Hannah's masochism, submission, and attempts at surrender (Ghent, 1990) must take center stage.

Novick and Novick (1987) describe masochism "as an *adaptation* to a disturbed environment" and "a *defense* against aggression" (p. 354). So in the face of a controlling and invasive mother (either only the mother is so powerful as to create this adaptation or the father's participation is left untheorized), the child uses herself, becoming the container for the mother's aggression. Using her own body to gratify the mother's needs sustains the mother as the idealized object. The "omnipotent aggression" (p. 367), experienced as such by the child who cannot yet symbolize and regulate it, must be turned against the self and not toward the mother. This turning against the self may take the form of beating fantasies or, I would add, relating to others who will literally or symbolically do the beating for you.

Certainly, Hannah grew up in a disturbed household where her mother's terrifying nightmares and "unpredictable moods" scared her and threatened to push her father out of the house. She writes, "I had never felt secure at home because mum was so unpredictable." Hannah had grown up with a model of anger not only being bad, but literally being "omnipotently" destructive, with the power to annihilate relationships. Additionally, she emerged in relation to a mother and father who were invasive and controlling, both using her body to gratify their needs. Her mother in particular was quite retaliatory, sadistically teasing, and taunting of Hannah. And again, Hannah's response to this environment included enough of her own "omnipotent aggression" that both her parents were required to hold her down to give her medicines. So Hannah grew up literally being pinned down and pried open. She was raised as a puppet to her parents.

Ghent (1990) claimed that some instances of masochism involve a "passionate longing to surrender" (p. 115). Ideally, surrender recalls Loewald's (1980) notion of eternity, where one "plunges into no-differentiation" (see also Milner, quoted in Ghent, 1990, p. 113) only to emerge more whole, more linked, more plumped up with meaning, and more vital. But submission and masochism can masquerade as surrender. Unlike the creativity of surrender, submission typically operates in the service of maintaining the status quo, reinforcing traumatic repetitions. Instead of the blissful, vitalizing unity of surrender, submission requires that one be a puppet to another.

A person who emerges from an environment of extreme

impingements "develops as an extension of the shell rather than of the core, . . . [the person] then *exists by not being found*" (Winnicott, quoted in Ghent, 1990, p. 117). These impingements become the sole organizing pattern around which one is able to relate to oneself and others. This pattern creates a model of self-regulation based on externally using the other as if he or she were a self-state. This complex maneuvering illustrates that masochism is not traumatic repetition in the service of mastering the original experience, but a desperate bid to integrate it (Ghent, 1990), to create meaningful temporal links, to resist the pattern of trauma. As Ghent notes, "The intensity of the masochism is a living testimonial of the urgency with which some buried part of the personality is screaming to be exhumed" (p. 116), penetrated, and recognized. Unfortunately, this desperation in the absence of faith in temporal linking results in submission.

Hannah grew up submitting to her parents. Given this "disturbed" environment of aggression and impinging control, Hannah may feel she needs to be in a relationship with a man who can physically and symbolically hold and contain her omnipotent, unorganized, unsymbolized anger, and not let it annihilate him—the idealized, merged-with other. This is submission in her quest to surrender. Indeed, when she is listing the qualities she wants in a man, she notes that he must be tall and bigger so she can "respect" him. She cannot feel safe enough to surrender unless her male partner is large enough to pin her down and save her from her own aggression. This is a classic case of Ghent's submission. Hannah's history of relationships supports his contention. As her diaries describe, she has had relationship after relationship with abusively penetrating people. So Hannah's seemingly masochistic participation in a sadistic relationship may be in part an attempt to keep her aggression from annihilating others and her self, and in part the only relational way she can feel recognized (Benjamin, 1995). [√] *[Hannah: temper in childhood anger—sarcasm—nothing]*[2]

But any discussion of masochism, submission, or surrender is incomplete without addressing the cultural inability to symbolize female anger

---

[2] Not only did her mother have a horrible temper, she was cruelly sarcastic to Hannah.

and aggression. Harris (1997) notes that girls fear their anger and aggression because they are not taught how to express and experience them. Thus, we have a transgenerational cycle of gendering by having indigestible omnipotent aggression passed from mother to daughter (Harris, 2005). This cycle can be broken only in relation to a nonsadistic parent who can contain and not retaliate against the child's unsymbolized aggression (Harris, 1997). Certainly male and female children alike benefit from this nonsadistic parent, but for girls this parent is key. As mentioned in Chapter 4, the culture creates many different avenues for male aggression to be digested, temporally linked, or acted out (albeit these avenues are not always healthy). The fields of competition and aggression are greatly limited for girls and generally take the form of self-destruction. Thus, experiencing and expressing aggression not only destroys relationships, it also threatens one's identity as a female in our culture. This cultural deficit, in addition to her family history, leaves Hannah with no space within which to hold or conceptualize her aggression.

So, for the adult Hannah, the dynamics of her marriage work to turn all her anger into an enactment of being the sick child. When she is angry, she vomits, attempts to overdose, or becomes upset and tearful. Eric then becomes the omnipotent parent who helps to maintain Hannah's location as the sick child and reinforces her inability to speak her anger. She can remain the infirm, helpless woman in relation to her powerful husband. The masochistic dynamics of her marriage help her to regulate her affect while they function to reinscribe her gender.

Given all that is hanging on Eric and Hannah's relational dance, it comes as no surprise that there is a high price to pay for disrupting their perfect rhythm. As Hannah writes of her marriage:

- If our relationship does not survive, I can't live without him so I must die. Truly believe now if family therapy does not work I am not worthy of living.

There seems to be a great deal of potential power being enacted by the masochist Hannah to keep sadist Eric on a pedestal. She is willing to die to maintain his status as the omnipotent parent. Having said this, I immediately want to take it back. If I acknowledge her power and control, am I saying she is asking for it? If so, I am enacting a relational analysis that I criticized in Chapter 2.

But, if I disavow her power and control, I leave her to be a helpless victim. Even couching these statements in the context of her history and bringing in a cultural analysis of female aggression still leave me treading dangerous misogynist waters, where the onus of change rests on Hannah's learning to symbolize her aggression "properly," as if that would end Eric's abusive behavior.

I can psychoanalytically examine masochism, sadism, submission, and control in Hannah's relationship to Eric, but these concepts all boil down to power, another term that is gendered male (Harris, 1997). To be powerful as a woman is to abnegate gender, a supposed core in one's identity. Within a patriarchal culture, women are literally named as the property of men, both as daughters and as wives. When Hannah married Eric, she said she knew she had to take his name and "obey" him. Indeed, obey was probably in the vows they took. In other words, Hannah's sadomasochistic relationships with men are the result of her familial disturbances, her desires to submit in an attempt to surrender, and her inability culturally to symbolize female anger. These relationships are supported by a culture that considers women the property of men; movies, books, and advertisements sexualize and romanticize women's suffering, martyrdom, and masochism, all of which make surrender a very tricky concept. After all, power and aggression can be gendered male only in relation to victimization, which is gendered female. One can surrender in the moment with a partner, but, if that partner has more power within the culture (based on identified gender, race, class, sexual orientation, etc.), then one is also necessarily submitting to them.

Throughout her own diary, von Sacher-Masoch (1990) described how she may have played the part of the sadist but only at the behest of the masochist, who nonetheless, in the end, held all the economic, social, and political power. Thus the tables were reversed, making him the sadist in control and her, the masochist, subject to his will. Within this cultural setup, surrender is also always submission for women. Culturally based power creates the space between, that is, the relationship; thus it, too, must be a subject of (psycho)analysis.

Hannah can lose herself within Eric, who will jump inside her to save her from her own experiences. Hannah submits to Eric's needs for dominance as Eric submits to Hannah's needs to be penetrated and controlled. While Hannah is being penetrated, symbolically and physically, by Eric, in the moment of penetration it is Hannah who suddenly may hold the power, while Eric, in the act of penetrating, is left momentarily vulnerable. He needs Hannah to penetrate.

Given this last addition to the analysis, however, we can see that their versions of submission are not equitable. Eric is seen as a male dominating a female in a patriarchal world, while Hannah is a female submitting to a male in the same patriarchal world.[3] Hannah's submissive role will always depend on her dissociating her capacities; Eric's will always depend on his dissociating his vulnerabilities. And while neither is particularly healthy, by playing the game, Eric gains status and power while Hannah must cautiously constrain hers and project it onto Eric. Eric's strength depends on and grows with Hannah's weakness, and he is willing to tie her up, hit her, colonize her body, to maintain this arrangement. And he can do this without police intervention or criminal charges of battery. She is his property. This tradeoff works so well because it follows the traditional cultural narrative of heterosexual relationships that temporally link vulnerable women with strong, heroic men and strong women with castrated men—the man's behavior (the effect) as the woman's responsibility (the cause).

The symbols through which women and men come into being as temporally linking people are those which teach women early to hide their strength and power in order to maintain their bonds with others, especially with men. This means that the position from which Hannah makes such choices about her behaviors is not at the same level of privilege and freedom as that from which

---

[3] Once again I am creating a false simplicity by focusing on gender to the exclusion of race, class, and ethnicity. One can see from this analysis just how complicated the power of race, ethnicity, class, and gender is relationally and how imperative it is to create the means to explore it. In this book, I have focused on gender, with the implicit, albeit often unwritten, understanding that Hannah is walking through what appears to be a white, upper middle-class British world, relationally constructed by a white, middle-class woman from the United States.

Eric chooses his behaviors. It may take two to tango, and her behavior necessarily affects and influences his, but relational equality is distorted, for she is always in high heels, dancing backward.

Although freedom of choice is a myth for both of them because their responses are generated from gendered, raced, classed pallets of potential relational interactions, he has the privilege of much wider freedom of movement both within their relationship and in the outside cultural world. In her relational world, Hannah may have a great deal of power, but her freedom of choice to express, experience, and relationally enact this power is severely constrained. Consequently, like her resistance, that lack of freedom most often is expressed in self-destruction, traumatic repetition, submission, and the creation of secrets. From these limited choices, her subjectivity is desperately awaiting recognition.

That Hannah is able to write about these interactions in her diaries is a significant shift in her capacity for temporal linking and hence differentiation. Indeed, at this point in the diaries, Hannah is beginning to question her dependence on Eric for her continuity. The woman who at the start of her diaries could not find her way home in her car decides to take a six-week holiday in the United States without Eric. She will visit her friend Meg (who at this point lives in New York City) and take an organized tour of the western United States. Eric will join her for the last two weeks, when they will drive up the eastern coast. This holiday is pivotal. It is during this first time away from Eric that Hannah is able to create usable space between them. She begins to question the health of their relationship. She wonders if she is happy being married to him.

But, as outlined in Chapter 2, if Hannah is to begin this process of separation she must create her own temporal links, which will bridge the otherwise unbearable space between herself and Eric. In the face of this differentiation (or furthering it), Hannah increasingly maintains her relational self-regulation through bulimia. With bulimia there is no capitulation to an other. As she wrote earlier of sex, she can do it herself just fine.

As we continue to follow Hannah's diaries, the entries begin to focus more and more on her newly created internal space, her capacity for. She now discusses actively bingeing and purging, fighting with Eric, actually experiencing desires separate from him—setting the stage for their eventual divorce. But this differentiation has some high stakes.

Chapter 7

Containing Her Self/Creating Temporal Links

Differentiation can be a dangerous proposition. In all her diaries, Hannah has used external bodies to create some sense of cause and effect. She has used others to contemplate the consequences of emotion and action, linking internal intentional states with external events, that is, temporal linking. As described earlier, without the capacity to safely contemplate cause and effect, a person cannot create the meaningful temporal links necessary to self-regulate, differentiate, and symbolize experience. In such a compromised state of development, one may use self-destructive violence to create these links (Fonagy and Target, 1998). This violence creates a form of self-regulation located solely on the body, where the only temporal links that can be created are those which are concrete and physical, literally visible on the skin (e.g., cutting) or through behaviors like bingeing and purging. Not surprisingly, with Hannah's differentiation from Eric comes a distinct shift in the way she uses bulimia as a form of temporal linking and self-regulation.

As Hoy (2004) describes, citing Foucault and Bourdieu, power is most successful when it is invisible, inevitable, and seen as natural. Again, we come into being through forms of culturally constructed cause and effect, temporal links. These links create the possibilities for our movements, our thoughts, our perceptions, and our experiences, but the particular power enacted to create each of us is always unique and changing. Thus, power, subjectivity, and resistance are always arising simultaneously in conscious and unconscious awareness. To resist these operations is to challenge the social structure as well as the structures of our own identities.

Hannah's identity has been formed by sadomasochistic enactments of power and domination. It is these dynamics that form her spine, her continuity. To shift this form of relationship is to question the very foundation of her identity. As she attempts to resist and open up the possibilities of her relationship with Eric, she simultaneously crumbles.

We know from the previous chapter that Eric provides an external form of temporal linking for Hannah. But this service comes at a high price of domination, manipulation, and control. But "freedom" from this control does not always appear to be healthier. Indeed, Hannah differentiates by self-destructing. This chapter tracks Hannah's gradual differentiation from Eric and her attempts at self-regulation in response to her growing sense of herself. These attempts take the form of escalating self-destructive behaviors, from bingeing and purging more frequently to her three attempts at overdosing, the second of which will land her in a public psychiatric hospital. It is during this hospitalization that Eric asks for a divorce and Hannah willingly complies. It is also after these overdoses that Hannah creates her future—starting her own very successful consulting business. This chapter takes us from her sixth adult diary to her eleventh.

Regulating Her Self Through Her Body

Using her body as a third in a triangle with Eric reenacts her parental relationship. Hannah's body was always used as an object for others to speak through and regulate their self-experiences. Now Hannah begins to shift from using Eric as a container to using her own body. Turning it into abject, greedy parts that need to be disciplined and perfected, she concentrates on her "fat thighs" and "upper arms," her "hips" and "abdomen." She also begins to split and objectify her "mind" into equally discrete components that need to be "worked on" in order to "develop" and "expand" her "taste in lit [literature], politics, history, and geography." She tries to revamp her appearance by changing her "clothes taste" and continually evaluates how well she is doing toward these goals (i.e., "coming on well now"). In the adolescent diaries she tacked the opinions of others onto her shell as if to create an experience of her self. Here she attempts to do this by splitting herself up into different, unintegrated pieces that can be perfected and then put together to construct a perfect experience that is no more than the sum of its dissociated parts. [√]

Timing the Constellations of Bulimia

The importance of bulimia for Hannah cannot be overemphasized. As the diaries relate, Hannah is not only beginning to recover memories of abuse, she is attempting to symbolize and integrate these memories. At the same time, she is also learning to experience her affective responses in order to differentiate. She does not have the luxury of beginning to experience herself as "real" within the holding environment of her mother's arms. She is learning to experience while moving as an adult through a complex, scary, and readily abusive world. The many behaviors surrounding bulimia provide a variety of holding in the face of this potential fragmentation and danger.

Creating Weighted Space to Hold Through Time

- Weighed and 107.58—really fluctuated from 107.14. Down from 110.4 but I am 101.2 on scales at home (103.4 naked here)[1]
- as soon as I went on the scales I was disappointed still 105.5 at home theref [therefore] at least 110 [at hospital]
- I just want to get home to weigh myself. I weighed myself at a shop yesterday and was 106. I want to be 100 but may be without clothes

---

[1] I converted her weights, originally written in kilos and stones, into pounds.

For Hannah, getting weighed is a mathematical process of calculating the subtle or not so subtle differences of each scale in each space. When Hannah is weighed at the hospital, she automatically calculates her weight at home and vice versa. There are differences on each scale in each space, so she appears to expand or shrink as she travels through space. Although the sense of her spatial continuity is challenged by these calculations, she can use the skin of numbers to hold her self. These numbers concretize the amount of space she takes up—her embodied volume. By measuring this embodiment from location to location, she creates a way of holding herself through space. In addition, because weight is a symbolic externalized representation of her body, she can project her self-experience into it, as she does with people. Weight can function as a third in a triangle with Eric, her mother, or herself in relation to her split-off body.

But this form of holding may also keep her from being fully in one space at any one time. When she is on holiday she wants to know her weight at home. When she is at home she imagines being at the hospital. When at the hospital she is calculating her weight at home. She is never fully in one place. Using weight in these ways both solidifies and challenges the experience of temporal stability. It provides an experience through which to hold on to her self through space but also keeps her from being fully embodied in one space at any one time.

- Weighed myself 108.4 in clothes–about same as last week. But 106.7 without sweatshirt (i.e., same clothes as Mon.) Higher weight official
- Weighed again 110. felt anxious about weight–even though in jeans and jumper–wanted to see how much clothes were. weighed myself with and without clothes and recon I'm lighter in nude on my scales then in clothes at hospital. That means I'm probably 103.6 instead of 104.9 when I was in a few weeks ago and after skiing. I looked at myself in mirror and studied the changes. I've put on weight so my bust looks bigger, my chest above bust doesn't show my ribs, my rib cage doesn't show as much and my face has filled out so my cheek bones don't show as much.
- Got weighed again–110.4. Exactly the same as on Mon. Felt angry-annoyed at the fact I haven't lost wt. despite being sick and restricting. wt. in pounds

is 104 in clothes—maybe that's not too bad. Means I'm probably still 103 naked which is the same as when I came in.

- Had wt.—106.7 so up from 105. Probably partly PMS as breasts feel really heavy

Weight also provides the skin to hold her self through time. As she struggles to differentiate from Eric, she is able to use weight as a way of holding on to her self from week to week. For instance, she can experience her 106 lbs. as being over 100 lbs. by measuring the space she takes up now in relation to the space she wants to take up in the future. That same figure, however, can measure the absented space she no longer takes up after having gone from 110 lbs. in the past to 106 lbs. in the present. Each weighing provides the opportunity to locate herself in space at that moment and to compare that weight with those throughout the previous weeks. Thus she creates a form of time, a concretized sense of going-on-being. She can even use weight to hold on to her self into the future by planning to lose weight. By her marking time and space in this way, weight provides a unit, a capacity for temporal linking.

Using weight for temporal linking while in treatment for bulimia has its costs and benefits. Within the treatment space, Hannah technically loses control over her weight. But by calculating her weight on different scales, she creates a way to play with space and time to regain control over her body. Being able to play and challenge her developing sense of continuity is important. As Winnicott (1971) noted, play is an activity that helps create a transitional space within which symbolic thought can be generated. Being able to figuratively travel and play in such paradoxes as reality–fantasy, inner–outer is integral to a person's being able to experience herself as "real."

As a trauma survivor with little sense of her self as being real, Hannah has created a safer, concrete space through which to travel symbolically. For instance, when she hits her target weight as defined by the hospital, she goes home to weigh her clothes to see what they added and then recalculates what she would have weighed in the hospital if she had been nude. This calculating reveals that technically she did not hit her target weight on every scale. She controls her temporality by shifting scales and units for temporal linking. She succeeds in regaining control over her body without having to purge or physically lose weight, for the moment.

This use of weight also keeps her from having to experience "being" (Winnicott, 1971) at any point in time. As we saw in the adolescent diaries, being can be dangerous for Hannah. She needed a triangulated form of relational linking to keep her ongoing experience of trauma in the past and present at bay. Given the split between her body and her mind, playing with weight, the externalized representation of her body, can enable her to resist this fragmentation and potential invasion. By maintaining and playing with this representation, she turns the unit of weight into a transitional object that is a symbol of her body. Thus, playing with weight may also foster mind–body integration. Obviously, the process of being weighed can be quite complex.

As it does with space, however, this way of playing with weight also provides a challenge to continuity through time. Hannah can gain or lose depending on her menstrual cycle. Her clothes can drastically alter her weight through time. As she notes, weight is not a constant unit; it is nothing to count on. It fuels the nagging sense of not really being sure she will continue to go-on-being while demonstrating that she will.

Varieties of Vomiting

- Felt full and didn't go out for walk. Kept regurgitating. Eventually felt too full and guilty for eating too much. Vomited a lot. Actually thought of writing feelings diary before it this time but was worried it might stop me vomiting and want to loose food and get the cleansing feeling of a vomit.

Exploring the meanings of purging is like opening Pandora's box. It is necessary to understanding bulimia, but it is not easy. Purging is an area where psychological theory, obscuring the political ideologies behind the rituals, has concealed women's embodied resistance. Diagnostic criteria and definitions of bulimia consistently describe purging as merely an attempt to lose weight and as a compensatory behavior after a binge. By being linked to the intentional prevention of weight gain, purging is conceptualized as existing only in relation to a binge. This connection frames the standard notion of purging and is problematic for a number of reasons.

First, it ignores the fact that women often go to great lengths just to purge. Many women binge in order to be able to purge. Others purge without bingeing at all. So purging itself must have its own very important meanings that are not dependent on bingeing.

Second, that definition perpetuates the stereotype that women self-destructively pursue vanity and that they purge to keep from disrupting the ideal of feminine beauty. Here it is accepted without question that no woman would want to gain weight, so, of course, they would purge the food they have just binged on. Purging becomes a normalized, essential ritual (Bourdieu, 1977) to remedy one's appetite's being out of control.

Certainly many patients with bulimia do claim they purge to prevent weight gain. Similarly, women with anorexia state that they are dieting because they are fat and need to lose weight. The expressed intentionality of the woman with anorexia is deconstructed, explored and identified immediately as a distortion. She is, after all, a skeleton who does not need to lose weight. But when women say they purge to prevent weight gain from a binge, their claim is accepted without question even though it too is a distortion. Basically, defining purging as the remedy to a binge normalizes violent self-destruction as a response to uncontrollable female appetite. This definition exemplifies the invisibility of a political ideology supporting rituals and cloaks both the physiological dangers of purging and the profound power and rage contained in it. Purging is a form of severe and powerful self-destruction and resistance. Only within a culture that actively patrols women's appetites (i.e., political ideology) can self-destruction masquerade as weight control (i.e., ritual) or can weight control justify self-destruction.

For Hannah, vomiting is not usually tied to a binge. Instead, it is the response to feeling "too full" after a "normal" (not a binge) meal, wanting to feel cleansed, or feeling anxious or upset. It is only once she has separated from Eric that she describes bingeing and then vomiting. Hannah uses vomiting in a variety of ways to resist and regulate relational contact with others or to regulate her own experiences.

Vomiting as Resistance to Invasion

- I apparently used to vomit when they [her parents] force fed me. I know I did the same with medicine—my parents hold me down and pinned arms down and forced my mouth open and shut and hold until swallowed. I outwitted and my will was stronger so I wouldn't swallow. I know whatever was wrong with me. I'd vomit. My throat was often raw with vomiting and I couldn't eat.

Hannah has been using vomiting to resist invasion and to control relational contact for most of her life. Indeed, according to the diaries, she vomited so much as a child she had ulcerated sores in her throat. *[Hannah: force-fed at school 7]*[2] Her thoughts, her clothes, her attitude toward her body, what and how much she ate were all under the strict and oftentimes confusing control of her triangularly warring parents. Vomiting allowed her to gain control over her body by expelling her parents and whatever substances they had forced down her throat.

Hannah's father was also bulimic. Hannah's bulimia may have functioned to keep him close to her, creating a relational triangle with Eric. But in her father's form of bulimia, vomiting and defecating were linked, perhaps even merged. Recall that he would go into the bathroom to vomit and use a glass rod to force himself to defecate. It seems there was a confusion or merging of orifices, which makes me wonder, if, when Hannah vomits, she is also symbolically defecating on Eric, her parents, and their respective forms of control over her.[3]

Furthermore, it is unclear whether her father also masturbated with the glass rod. Certainly, given the invasive cloud of sexual invasion that hung over Hannah's interactions with her parents,

---

[2] She said she was force fed by the school nurse when she would not eat lunch at school. I do not know exactly what that entailed.

[3] I thank Adrienne Harris for this observation.

it is not far-fetched to imagine that in addition to the orifices of mouth and anus, those which are often involved in orgasm—vaginas and urethras—are also collapsing and merging here. Purging could be a way of returning to that state of being where there is absolutely no differentiation between inner and outer, as all boundaries (e.g., orifices of in–out) are exploded through the violent act of vomiting. Vomiting may involve both shitting and cumming on others, saying fuck you at the same time as regressing to a state of total helpless nondifferentiation.

Vomiting also has a great deal of significance in her relationship with Eric. When Eric finds out Hannah is bulimic, he makes her "promise I'd always tell him if I wanted to vomit." Unlike her mother, he does not tell her not to vomit, but to tell him if she feels as though she wants to vomit. This is an insidious form of control. He is not content merely to hand down a declaration, "Do not vomit again." Instead he must be in her head, knowing what she knows, knowing what she does, feeling what she feels. When she wants to vomit she must tell him so that he knows and can symbolically be with her if she still vomits. Penetrating her main defense of vomiting, which she uses to resist those who try to penetrate her, he leaves her impotent to fight his invasion.

But instead of complying by telling him or hiding it as a secret as she did with her mother, Hannah stops vomiting altogether. She gives Eric the equivalent of the "silent treatment" by refusing to vomit, refusing to "speak" in the language he has invaded. Instead she begins regurgitating her food—partially swallowing it, then bringing it back up into her mouth, and then partially swallowing it again. She adapts her vomiting behavior with Eric by regurgitating secretly at the table with him, in front of him, before she swallows the food he is forcing her to eat. This takes to a new level the violent aggression of throwing her parents up and out of her. It is a brilliant adaptation for her passive–aggressive attempts to resist invasion and to insert herself into their relationship and into her own body. By doing it at the table, she is not only challenging Eric's control, she is outright humiliating him and rendering him impotent.

Of course, this power play is kept entirely secret. As Collins (1990) notes, secret thoughts are still a powerful form of resistance in the face of colonization. Khan (1993) considered secrets an important space to encapsulate the self. For Hannah, regurgitation served both purposes as well as that of aggressively striking back at Eric. The only problem with this take on her vomiting is that, if vomiting overlaps with defecating, she is also swallowing shit in order to resist his control. *[Hannah: regurgitate as silent revenge]*[4]

Hannah begins vomiting again soon after she and Eric are married. One of the ways she uses vomiting is to punish herself and Eric. For instance, when Eric tells her she does not have a nice figure, she responds:

- I felt silent and sad. Thought maybe better if I wasn't here—less hassle E'd be happier. Bad day eating. Preoccupied with food. Even thinking of buying a calorie counter. A little sick after lunch [vomited]—rejection [E's comment about her body]? Exercised before bath and pushing my body on walk. Sick after desert and only ate half rest back in [toilet] bowl. Sick after cheese and biscuits too.

There Eric has criticized her body and she is "silent and sad." She does not write of being angry at him. She feels suicidal and vomits after each course of her meal with him. She herself ties her vomiting to his comment when she asks herself if her motivation is related to his "rejection." Again, vomiting may help her to get his comment and her feelings about his comment out of herself, but it is also more significant. Vomiting is perfectly suited to their sadomasochistic relationship because it is a self-destructive behavior that is also pointedly an expression of anger toward Eric. He sadistically attempts to control her body on many different levels, and she masochistically–sadistically resists by vomiting and planning to diet, ostensibly getting rid of her body. If he does not appreciate her body, then she will get rid of it and he will not be able to have it to control. By abusing her own body in this way, she is able to express anger toward him for hurting her while simultaneously punishing herself for being angry at her omnipotent parent, who must remain powerful for her own stability.

Clearly, vomiting for Hannah is not one definable behavior. It can be a rebellion against colonization, complicity, evacuation

4 Using the term revenge, she agreed with this assessment.

of feelings, or a sadomasochistic flip where Hannah, the angry party, can turn her anger against herself to hurt both herself and Eric. And when all else fails, in a pinch she can regurgitate instead of vomiting, swallowing the shit but rejecting Eric's control.

Vomiting to Regulate Self-Experience

- Today much more jumpy about food. Actually vomited a little as I was about to leave and on way to tube. Probably anxiety about being weighed
- Today feel depressed and ate cake and vomited. A pattern?
- Quite sad and anxious in session—all my nails are bitten down again. I seem to be on the border of getting better or getting worse. continued about anxiety and the 'getting better' issue. Remembered biscuits from this morn and ate 2. Later went out waiting room and ate 2 more. Then off the toilet to be sick
- Went home and saw shape of my stomach and had to vomit
- After Sue's I was so desperate to be sick I got myself stuck in a field—but the compulsion to vomit was so intense I had to get off the road
- On the Sat I went w/Fran to her family. I was feeling fat before I went, but started with a beer over lunch and even though no one else drank it was a bad start. I felt greedy. I gave the kids their presents but ate a few sweets and kept back 2 bags of milky way balls. I got on the bus and scoffed a bag of chocolate and spent the rest of the journey throwing up very discreetly into a bag.

Hannah also uses vomiting to regulate her own self-experiences. In all but the last entry, the "compulsion to vomit," as she calls it, is unrelated to overeating. Instead she ties it to feeling anxious. She is worried about getting weighed, so she vomits. She is worried about getting better or worse, so she eats a biscuit in order to vomit. She sees her stomach, so she vomits. After two social situations, she needs so intensely to vomit she gets her car stuck in a field and another time just vomits in public on the bus. The compulsion to vomit is so strong that she cannot even wait to get home from a social event. She cannot regulate her affective experience in order to travel home. She must get it out of herself on the way.

Vomiting here seems to be a desperate and necessary act that allows her to throw up and throw out her affective experiences, and they are expelled before they can even be labeled. Other than the general descriptive "anxious," I have no idea what she is feeling that needs to be evacuated so immediately. And, given the level of desperation she describes, this form of regulation is imperative to her functioning. As these entries demonstrate, purging really is a phenomenon separate from bingeing; it has its own intentionality and expression. Not only are there different meanings to vomiting, there are different forms, each of which create a particular potential space of resistance and reenactment.

Bingeing and Differentiation

Regulating her self-experience becomes even more complicated when Hannah separates from Eric. It is here, in the 11th adult diary that Hannah begins mentioning bingeing.

- Dinner—cod in sauce: carrots; Ate standing up. Rest of packet dipped in lemon curd. Rest of mousse choc. Tea. Felt chaotic and a binge
- I'm feeling sad, lethargic and unmotivated. Having had an excellent time with Patty for 4 1/2 days, I now feel lonely . I'm tired and feel fat. I left the house fairly empty of food when they arrived but have eaten much more with them here. The gave me 4 [cakes] and 2 rolls to take to work and of course I ate 3 on the bus and polished off the rolls before lunch. Lunch of pizza finished me off. I'm already thinking of the food they left—crisps and strudel. I want to eat it and throw up. Yesterday just on the way to meet them I crammed in an ice cream and 2 cakes. Dinner was huge and I felt no hunger and no fullness—just wanted to cram in more food.
- I want to eat and throw up. I feel quite tearful as I think of my messy life. I feel so empty and alone.

Bingeing, like purging, serves a particular function for Hannah. As mentioned, she did not write often about bingeing until she was separated from Eric. During her marriage, when she is constantly being invaded by Eric, she is desperately trying to get him and her experiences out of her body as quickly as possible. She cannot have anything inside her. She does not like to eat or even to hold her urine, as absenting her physical body is primary. After their separation, she seems desperately to fill up, to take things in, and even though she does not always vomit it back up, it is unclear how much is being integrated.

In the diaries written during her marriage, Hannah rarely mentions having friends. As is typical in abusive relationships, Eric believes she should need only him. As she separates from him, she begins to have contact with friends. This contact is often linked to bingeing. When Hannah is in Prague during an eight-week consulting job, two friends visit her. She describes having dinner with them and wanting to eat everything and just "cram in the food." When they leave, she eats in one sitting all the leftovers they bought together. After spending years expelling people, she is desperate to ingest them. This shift is very important. For her to need or want to incorporate others, she must be starting to have a sense of self and other, differentiation. She must be experiencing the beginnings of her own experience as a separate person, and this experience indicates emptiness and aloneness. She is not embodied by someone else or using another to live through. Instead, she uses food to concretize the bridge, the temporal link, in order to maintain contact while differentiating.

- Since these relationships [during her separation she had sexual relationships with 3 men] I have eaten a lot more—all cakes and sweets, ice cream and bread—what I normally don't eat. The first 2 weeks (preman) were fine—normal balanced eating. Since then chaotic to a greater or lesser degree. I currently can't always be bothered to make myself sick or a token gesture

Hannah also uses food to deal with her experiences of having sex with three different men while she is in Prague. Although she does not describe her feelings about them, she notes that her eating became "chaotic," and she was eating foods she did not usually eat. Eating is the key behavior here, for as she notes, she could not even be bothered to take the time to vomit. While she vomited Eric out of her, here she takes in the man and sits with her fullness and discomfort. This is a new capacity.

For the first time Hannah also tries to understand her interactions with these men. She begins by noting that she was unable to say no to one of them, just as in her past encounters. But then she ends one entry, "Wonder what message I'd given to deserve such attention." Here she actually tries to create a cause and effect for the sexual encounter. It is important that the first temporal explanatory link she creates is one that mirrors the culture by giving her the sole responsibility for the encounter. However, as she is making space for a sexual relationship that is not based exclusively in the masochistic–sadistic other, it may be important that she create meaning by taking responsibility and retaining control for the encounter. She may not have been able to say no, but she also may have unconsciously invited him to approach her. This temporal linking may help to keep her from experiencing the recent relationship as a direct reenactment of her previous abuses. Shifting the repetition in this way also enables her to gain the distance necessary not only to observe her own behavior, but also perhaps to begin to recognize potentially threatening and abusive behaviors in others before the enactment is in full swing.

Whatever was triggered for her in these encounters, her capacities to deal with it were significantly different from how she described relationships previously. Just as she describes wanting to take in rather than expel, she also describes being "chaotic" and out of control. Vomiting is a form of resistance and gaining control. Here Hannah is demonstrating a new-found ability to experience herself being out of control. This is such a profound shift in the diaries because it indicates that she is not successfully dissociating and is actually beginning to feel. Note the terms she uses to describe her self-experience in these entries: "sad, lethargic and unmotivated," "tearful," "lonely, and "empty." These are descriptions of deep emotional experiences. They are not terms Hannah has used in the past. She is no longer the empty shell devoid of emotional experience, nor is she exclusively vomiting experience out of herself. She is feeling and learning to experience, linking her binges with her feelings of despair. She is creating links of intention and action—temporal linking. She is internalizing her experiences, indicating the creation of a capacity for, a subjectivity through which she is making meaning for the first time.

Here we see how Hannah is able to use bulimia to incorporate or expel orally, depending on the capacity she needs. When she relies exclusively on externalization, she is able to vomit; when she is beginning to hold experiences, she is able to binge without purging. Both enable her to regulate relational access and contact with others while she regulates her self-experience and is attempting to differentiate from others. Bulimia becomes a temporal link creating and bridging the space between. Through bulimia, she can begin to create herself while she creates others.

The High Embodied Stakes of Differentiation

- Whenever I wake up in the night I have to go to pass urine. I don't seem to be able to cope w/ any sensation of pressure/water in me and have to go even though often not a full bladder. When I wrote this I nearly put water in my stomach that was the thought but I know intellectually it's incorrect. I have a real problem w/passing water—often I can't hold it until I find a toilet and have to just pee in a car par, etc. Sometimes I'll wet myself—I can't hold it in. I know Dad used to go to pass urine frequently—like me he'd go in anticipation of an inability of being able to go for a while e.g. long walk etc. It used to irritate mum and I'd copy her (I'D GET MAD AT HIM TOO). Even farts I can't hold in. I sometimes get IBS [irritable bowel syndrome—excessive gas and diarrhea] and am not sure now which is which again [she is having difficulty differentiating needing to pass gas from needing to move her bowels]. I can't hold in wind etc. and have to get rid of it immediately. Recently at work as I was so unsure of sensation—fart or wanting to excrete—I crapped in my pants. Had to clean myself up and felt embarrassed and now I worry I don't know different sensations

As we saw in Chapter 2, aspects of differentiation surround eating. Similarly, Hannah's differentiation initially revolves around bulimia. As the child differentiates, other aspects of the body become important sites for experiencing self and other, inner and outer, and creating temporal links of cause and effect, in particular through toilet training. So perhaps it is not surprising that, as Hannah differentiates from Eric, she also struggles with incontinence. Ironically, with all Hannah's work methodically and meticulously to piece her body together, she loses control of one of the earliest ways we can control our body.[5] Like a child, Hannah can-

[5] During the collaboration Hannah elaborated on this incontinence as being primarily due to weaning herself off laxatives and diuretics. Taking

not differentiate needing to pass gas from having to move her bowels, a confusion that causes her to excrete in her pants. Integral to differentiating from others is the capacity to differentiate her own embodied experiences, which is not easy for Hannah, especially as an adult.

Hannah seems to be floating in that transitional space between being inhabited by Eric, who would provide a container for her experiences, and having to learn to regulate and experience her body by herself. Hannah is a woman who has never learned to experience when she needs to eat, what she wants to wear, what she desires. As a space opens between Eric's control and her own body, she begins to make connections with her embodied experience. But this body has spent its life being sadistically controlled by parents or men, so that attempting to contain it with her newly formed capacity to create temporal links is like learning to drive by steering an 18-wheeler. She needs an owner's manual for her body. [√√]

As Hannah is struggling to differentiate self from other, inner from outer simultaneously and concretely through food, controlling when it goes in and when it comes out becomes essential. To exercise this control successfully, the body is reduced to two functions: eating and excreting, ignoring or bypassing the process of digestion. These behaviors once again link Hannah to her father. He made himself vomit with a toothbrush to "cleanse" himself, and Hannah often craves the "cleansing feeling of a vomit." Both Hannah now and her father then are engaged in a power struggle over their respective anal and oral desires. The result is a reduction of both their bodies into two holes that must be kept clean and free of food and desire. But, unlike in the past, when her oral aggression and anal sadism were dissociated, projected into others, and acted out unconsciously through bingeing and purging,

---

laxatives and diuretics can affect the phenomenological feeling of urgency to urinate, defecate, or pass gas. By attempting to end her abuse of these pills, she was still struggling to regulate oral and anal, in and out. In the diaries, Hannah rarely mentions taking these pills, and she did not use them for periodic purging to substitute for vomiting. They do indicate the extent to which she controlled each orifice—mouth, anus, and urethra.

here Hannah is beginning to experience them, even while she knows they are too strong for her to control.

Hannah's increasing capacity for integration may be best exemplified by her having had an accident in her pants at work. Work is the one area where Hannah seems to flourish unbridled. There are only three entries about work in these diaries, and in each entry she speaks confidently, assuredly, and with a distinct sense of her own subjectivity. This proportion of entries stands in contrast to that in her adolescent diaries, where she virtually ignores her chaotic and abusive home life in favor of focusing on school, the site of her academic achievements. Containing her competent public self in the adolescent diaries and her traumatized bulimic child-self exclusively in the adult diaries allows her to maintain the distinct split between these two aspects of her self.

This split is challenged when she describes "crapping in her pants" at work. This accident violates the most important boundary protecting the public adult from the messy memories of trauma indicating that her dissociative processes are either crumbling or being dismantled. Not only is she less and less able to manage the separation between her embodied child persona and her clean, organized work persona, but the traumatized, split-off, ignored child basically "crapped" all over the adult. Through her incontinence, the rage of Hannah's screaming child is beginning to be seen.

Overdosing to Kill the Child Once and for All

As Hannah begins to integrate these explosive aspects of herself, while she is creating the capacity for self-experience and temporal linking and is beginning to differentiate from Eric, it seems inevitable that her attempts simultaneously to resist, control, and submit will escalate. This internal tug of war culminates in the 11th adult diary, in which she describes attempts to overdose three times. Hannah first attempts by using antidepressants when she has been alone, separated from Eric for the first time while she is traveling through the United States. This entry occurs after he has joined her for a short holiday.

- I feel quite drunk after drinking 1/2 bottle of wine. I've just had a long conversation with E. and ended up in tears after feeling the disloyal ungrateful part of the relationship. He mentioned divorce—in the context of if that's what I want. Yet how can I choose? I can only see nothing—I have no gut feelings. Took 9 days of anti-depressants—maybe I'll change. 1:30 am first realization was that I had actually woken up—quite resigned to the fact that I would not

As the "ungrateful" partner, Hannah can see no way out but to overdose. And while she makes the attempt, she indicates paradoxically that she does not expect to live but also expects to change. Embodied experience gives the world meaning, as the world imbues embodied experience with meaning (Merleau-Ponty, 1962). With no capacity to generate this cycle of meaning, Hannah is unable to know herself or Eric. The overdose violently coheres her and creates the space within which to accumulate and experience. Hannah writes, "I have no gut feelings." She is suddenly able to access and create the capacity for an interior space or gut-generating experience, and it is empty. This space becomes a presence through a genuinely affective experience of emptiness, "no gut feelings."

After that attempt, Hannah begins to express not only her distress over the fight and her relationship with Eric, but also her desire to change. With too many antidepressants in her system, she spends the night sitting on a dock and watches the sunrise. She is jittery, exploring her life and what she desires. Writing of her relationship at a deeper level than before, she notes the changes in herself, how easy it was to be with her friend Meg, and how difficult it is to be with Eric.

- I don't understand why I can't naturally be like with E. humorous, free spontaneous, etc. as I was on my tour and with Meg. I seem to be getting more and more into new age ideas—veg [vegetarianism], ecology, environment, self astrology, palmistry. very different from Eric's scientific views

It is no wonder she is feeling the ungrateful partner. For the first time, Hannah actually has views, ideas, her own thoughts; and they are directly contradictory to those of Eric. He has been dethroned as the omnipotent parent. But can she exist without one?

That attempt at overdosing is followed by another, more serious one shortly after Hannah and Eric return to London. The second attempt also follows a conflict with Eric, this time during family therapy, when Hannah was unable to tell Eric how she felt about his arriving in the United States after she had been there on holiday without him for a few weeks. She writes:

- I can't believe I'm so sad as I write this. We've just had a session with Lili. It must have been awful for E. to listen to the long pause after Lili's question as to what I was excited about in E's pending arrival. I feel I'm going to leave a decision in God or fates hands. If I live then maybe we will or maybe we won't work things out. But if I don't live, it was not meant to be. At least most people don't know we've had any problems and could just think I was depressed. I don't want people to think I was depressed because of E. I can't believe how hard it is to swallow these pills. My body is so thin it feels like they show through. I could see my veins and muscles on my body as I dressed this morning.
- I hope this does not cause more pain and harm. I just want to stop hurting everyone. I feel so guilty. I'm causing upset and I'm still not happy.

The prose part of the entry is followed by an exploration list, a rune reading of her future about what she needs to do.[6] This list addresses her marriage, "partnership—achieved only by separateness"; the potential for change, "Strength—termination and new beginnings. Opportunity disguised as loss. May require death in myself"; and her need to have patience, "Harvest—no quick results. Cannot hurry the harvest."

There are many important points to make about this disturbing entry. Clearly this overdose is much more serious than the previous one. She describes seeing her veins and muscles while she is taking the pills, and the distinction between inner and outer seems to have completely disintegrated, leaving her as a walking inner with no outer, no container within which to hold her self. Everyone can see and has access to her insides. Now she also knows

[6] Rune readings—an ancient Celtic form of fortune telling—are something Hannah has done throughout the adult diaries.

she has an inner because she can see it. She is no longer covered in Eric's skin. She knows she exists and has "gut feelings" because she has seen her muscles and veins showing through her own skin.

This overdose may be indicative of the moment when the abused child self surrenders to the abusive parent. But taking herself out of the process entirely through death is also the final act of taking control over the parental abuser. Here Hannah will do the deed once and for all, and, by killing herself, she is doing the deed better than the parent did. She is taking the "omnipotent control" of the devastating experience that Winnicott (1971) described as being necessary to let the past heal the present. Of course, here again is a paradox, as taking control through a suicidal act also potentially kills the future.

Overdosing may be a powerful communication to both Eric and her parents. She would leave Eric with the knowledge and burden of a wife who committed suicide and also with numerous diaries that tell more of the story than that to which Eric has been privy. And this overdose, like the previous one, seems to have been precipitated by Hannah's feeling that she cannot speak what she feels in family therapy. In the first overdose she describes seeing "nothing" and having "no gut feelings." Yet she describes something, for she notes that she does not know how to choose whether or not she wants a divorce. Even to write the word divorce indicates that much internal shifting is occurring.

This last overdose, as she describes, was the outcome of "the fact that I couldn't say what I wanted to Lili's question. I also felt I'd never have the nerve to face E. and say what I really wanted to or needed to." Even though Hannah spoke the only language she knew—abusing her body—she writes as if she actually did know what she wanted to say but just could not say it in the presence of Eric. Here is another huge shift. She knows what she wants and can write it in words; she just cannot say it in relation to Eric. Instead, she chooses her usual body language, and it says it very clearly for her that she does not want to live with Eric.

If self-mutilation and pain can be cohering for the self, providing a way of linking intention and action (Fonagy and Target, 1998), then this overdose seems to have created a new self for

Hannah. As her rune reading indicated, opportunity "may require death in myself." While she is in intensive care, she continues writing in her diary. She is suddenly able to make a decision to start her new business. She also writes for the first time that she does not think she loves Eric any more. It seems that something quite significant shifted in the process of her overdose.

The last two entries are also disturbing because they illustrate textually what Davies and Frawley (1992, 1994), Knoblauch (1997, 2000), Bromberg (1998), Layton (1998), and Harris (2005) describe as multiple simultaneous yet unintegrated interactions, and these interactions are about life and death. As Hannah is swallowing pills to kill herself, she is writing in her diary about the experience! It is as if the experience can occur only if she holds it within the diaries. And once she is in intensive care she continues her plans about her future. There is a weird logic here that I find hypnotizing, and I continually have to pull myself out in order to remember that she is planning for the future while she is discussing the pain of swallowing pills, while she is discussing her overwhelming past, while she is trying to kill herself. The conflation of time here is stunning and disturbing. Different experiences and times are converging on her at once, and only the experience and act of overdosing is potent enough to help her find her self, mark the spot where she temporally stands so that she can then move forward. And, indeed, she is suddenly able to make many difficult decisions about her future.

Overdosing seems to have served multiple purposes. First, Hannah created relational distance between herself and Eric as she was beginning to feel her intolerable experiences of not loving him. She also seemed to regulate her self in a familiar way by self-abuse, but this time she actually became the ultimate omnipotent parent as she almost killed the child entirely. But, perhaps most important, this form of self-abuse helped her locate herself temporally. Through an extreme form of self-mutilation and pain she identified her place in space and time and could begin to move forward.

Having said that, I should emphasize that these attempts were just that, attempts. The first appeared to be relatively minor;

and, although the second landed her in the emergency room, Hannah was able to continue writing in her diary during and after. Hannah does attempt one more overdose shortly after that one. The third attempt is very serious. The diaries contain only a mention of it after the fact as the event that leads to her second hospitalization. I know the details only from our collaboration. She told me that she took sleeping pills, went to bed next to Eric, and woke him later in the night with her seizures. This was the only attempt for which she was hospitalized, and this time she was placed in a public psychiatric hospital. Eric decided she was telling him something through her overdose, and he asked for a divorce.

Aron and Harris (1993), citing Ferenczi, note that "resistant" action is essential to the transformation of traumatic experience. Indeed, because oppression is carved into our muscles, resistance must be embodied action if it is to be transformed (Sampson, 1996). This conceptualization situates resistance in the paradoxical space where transforming potentials exist. However, one can resist trauma and violence by resisting growth or life itself. Labeling resistant behavior as subversive or traumatic repetition can convey a great deal of power to either the analyst or the patient. Here the question is not where embodied activity switches from traumatic repetition to subversive repetition but, rather, how they are cooccurring, and which aspects of resistance are most alive relationally in the moment. In her attempts to overdose, Hannah creates a space for the only form of action she can take to transform her life. As she writes, "Opportunity is disguised as loss: may require death in myself."

We have seen that self-destructive behavior is situated in a particular relational matrix. The behaviors of bulimia—vomiting and bingeing—are important forms of self-regulation and regulating relational contact, but they are also forms of communicating. As Hannah begins teasing herself out from within Eric's very limiting membrane, her forms of communication change. She shifts from regurgitation to vomiting, then to losing or gaining control by bingeing and through incontinence. As she writes, she attempts suicide when she is unable to communicate what she wants to say to Eric. So she relies on her body to do this communicating for her—and it works.

But Hannah's self-destructive behaviors are not only a sign of her inability to communicate, they also indicate that, until this point, Eric has not had the capacity to listen. While her overdoses are her last-ditch efforts to get the message across to Eric, they also signal that he is just not listening to what she is saying. As with forms of political resistance, the more the action is ignored, the more disruptive resistance must become. Here Hannah must attempt suicide three times before Eric finally gets the message that she wants a divorce. Fortunately, she gets the message as well.

The last overdose becomes in the adult diaries what Hannah's response to Karen's letter was in the adolescent diaries. And, as in the adolescent diaries, this event comes and goes with barely a mention. This three-dimensional apex, however, does not lead to an emotional desert. Instead, Hannah is able to blossom from her near-death suicide attempt. She and Eric divorce, and she begins a very successful business. She meets a new partner, Mark, with whom she has a less abusive relationship. Once able to begin to experience her present, Hannah is able to recreate her past. She does this in her last diary, which is almost exclusively composed of lists. To finish this story, we must turn to how Hannah structures her text and how she ends her diaries in lists.

Chapter 8

Creating Bodies in the Text

> We cannot discuss our way out of oppression when that oppression is embodied, carved into the muscles and retained in the body's knowledge of its place in the world . . . the actual body is molded to carry within its very tissues and muscles the story of ideology. Given the depth to which embodied ideological practices have penetrated and remain deeply secreted within us, I am talking about a very difficult area for transformation, one that cannot be changed by thought alone but only by embodied action [Sampson, 1996, pp. 620–621].

In this chapter we pull Hannah's adult diaries and the analysis together by focusing on how she improvisationally plays with the structure of her text so as to contain dissociated aspects of her self in different textual spaces. To do this, we go back in time to explore the structure of all her 13 adult diaries.

As we know, merely remembering trauma can be retraumatizing on many levels. First, if trauma disrupts temporality, then remembering the past means the event is relived in the present. Second, the discursive frames making meaning of temporal linking for survivors are imposed from outside by numerous different "experts" (Foucault, 1972). Because survivors are not able to create their own ways of communicating trauma, their experiences are constrained by others. This constraint can serve as a second invasion, which is magnified when the frames of meaning-making are victim blaming. Third, creating an integrated temporal existence requires melding time and space, mind and body. When memories of abuse are contained within embodied experiences, the process of recontacting the body and mind can be frighteningly retraumatizing. Additionally, the cultural denigration of bodies (female bodies in particular) and suspicion of embodied experience further renders such integration potentially retraumatizing.

Absent the capacity for a sense of agency, cause and effect—in other words, time—self-destructive violence can often be the only way to link internal intentional states with external events (Fonagy and Target, 1998). Self-destructive violence like bingeing and purging or engaging in violent relationships enables one to create concrete, exclusively bodied temporal links that help to order but not to symbolize experience. This form of temporal linking can regulate overwhelming affect to some degree.

To create the temporal links necessary to interrupt this self-destruction, one needs to be able to access the experiences of the body. Given Hannah's tendency to dissociate her embodied experience, she (like most trauma survivors) is caught in a never-ending cycle of self-destruction. After all, these dissociated states form a multiplicity of experiences that are ongoing in the moment (Davies and Frawley, 1992, 1994; Knoblauch, 1997, 2000; Bromberg, 1998; Harris, 2005). These relational forms of violence are everywhere.

In the diaries, Hannah finds a way to circumvent these issues by creating her own discursive frames that reflect the multiplicity of her experiences. The diaries provide a snapshot of multiplicity on the page. In so doing, she creates her first primarily expansive form of resistance by defying the constraining traumatic repetition that is typically inevitable in the telling of one's story. As she describes traumatic events, she can place a memory safely into a movie—she can write as if she were describing scenes for filming. She can write it as dialogue for a play where each participant is tethered to his or her assigned lines. She can contain her memories within the multiple, shifting self-states that may take turns speaking in one paragraph. Or she can write her experience as a list.

Creating all these flexible textual bodies through which to construct temporal links becomes the key to interrupting self-destruction. With these textual options, she can shift from prose, to lists, to movies, to diagrams, to plays, back to prose again, demonstrating the ingenious flexibility of creating bodies in her text and the importance of such transitional and "transgressive spaces" (Alcoff and Gray, 1993) in healing.

The most intricate and varied way Hannah uses the text is by her creation of lists. Hannah created 82 lists in the diaries; they constitute approximately 40% of the text. *[Hannah: stunning]*[1] This percentage rises in the last diary, which is composed almost entirely of lists. These lists beautifully outline the process of cleavage and differentiation described in Chapter 2. They also provide an interesting example of how multiplicity can be expressed dynamically on a page. So far, the analysis of her adult diaries has been only of the content of her prose. Through this aspect of her text, we have seen her gradually differentiate from Eric and, in the process, wind herself tightly around bulimic behaviors and suicide attempts until she begins to create a life of her own. But how she actually achieves this remains unclear.

Before we close her diaries and this book, allow me to retell this important story, but through the structure of her text, the evolution of her lists. As mentioned in the first chapter, Hannah's story is told through the content and the process of her text reflected in its structure. Focusing on the structure of her text—her textual body—provides the missing "link" to her story of transformation, which is how she creates embodied temporal links. This story, held in the structure of her text, is a step-by-step guide to how she created time. While each of these steps is dynamic and

---

1 Hannah was stunned by the number of lists in her diaries. She had thought her use of lists was a relatively recent adaptation.

inextricable, they are separated here for illustration. I begin where she begins:

Steps Toward Cleavage

Hannah initially appears only as an undifferentiated blob of words, conflated with her mother and Eric. Here the diary itself was the only skinned boundary. There is no "I" or "me," no differentiated time. For a reader, the text is a morass of confusing events with no sense of directed movement, action, or experience. It is impossible to tell who is doing what to whom. The first list emerges from this textual density to create a body from undifferentiated prose. This body houses Hannah, her mother, and Eric. While the three constitute one list, triangulation develops as a form of gaining relational distance, indicating the beginning of a cleavage/differentiation process. The list appears when she is discussing how Eric has invaded her boundaries. She notes that there are "interesting parallels" between how Eric and her mother treated her. Alternating line by line one incident from Eric and one incident from her mother, Hannah creates a buffering triangle (see Table 1).

Memorial processes involve internalizing traces of the object (Loewold, 1980). Hannah manages to moderate potential contact with her abusive objects by creating an externalized space within which to develop this memorial process. In this externalized space, she titrates both her mother's and Eric's appearances

TABLE 1: The Buffering Triangle
M tied up with scarf in room when child
E. tied up with tie by radiator for sex
M inserted tampax in me with legs apart when 13
E. puts cream on my bottom with legs apart
M smacked me if naughty
E. slipper used to spank.

by alternating lines. This simultaneously regulates her memories of abuse by ensuring that only individual lines of each memory emerge at one time.

But in these initial lists, no one person has a definable body, a situation that is both positive and negative. First, because they do not have differentiated bodies, there is no definable moment or site of invasion. There is no distinct point on the page where her mother's or Eric's body is separate from the other and able suddenly to penetrate Hannah's. It helps that Hannah's body is virtually absent. She appears only as the implied site of abuse within lines of a list. Here, when need be, she can excise herself from the action by creating the absent subject of the list. She is present for her mother to "smack" her, but she writes herself out when Eric spanks her. She is able to control the location and structure of the memory (in a diary and a list) and can decide whether or not she wants to participate in the interaction this time around.

However, as one undifferentiated body, her mother and Eric are also one undifferentiated memory of abuse. Remembering one automatically conjures up the other, undoubtedly overwhelming Hannah's experience in the moment. Here her past is her present.

As the diaries progress, however, Hannah begins to tease out her mother's abuses from Eric's until they are two distinct parts of one list (see Table 2).

She creates a vertical chronology, writing "mum" and a list of abuses, then with no spatial break she writes "Eric," and lists his abuses. While the two still reside in one list, producing one large body, and Hannah's body is still an absent site of abuse, this body housing her mother and Eric is beginning to have some differentiation through the creation of succession. Like a cell undergoing mitosis, her lists are beginning to divide.

The lists following this one represent her mother's and Eric's successful division, and the two never again appear within the same list. Instead, her mother and Eric have separate, parallel bodies, in separate lists. The appearance of these bodies in separate spaces signals a new creation of temporality. There is now a past marked in space by her mother and then Eric's differenti-

TABLE 2 Dividing Mum and Eric

With mum I had:
no privacy
no secrets until I left home to marry E. except in anorexic phase
obedience
no anger, sarcasm
high degree of control
no relationship w/dad
fulfilled her dreams and career aspirations
become the body shape she wanted
With E. I have:
no privacy
no secrets
total obedience
punishment and reward
confidence to succeed
no anger
little self confidence
always put myself last
am his conversation and bubbly and smiling
wear clothes he likes
have hair cut he likes
have a young underdeveloped body
am passive sexually
broken some links with mum
became some religion
am nothing on my own so won't ever leave

ated bodies. Using this newly created temporal space, Hannah's body emerges on the page.

Interestingly, at this point in the diaries her father's body also appears for the first time (see Table 3). The appearance of her father maintains a form of triangulation within the lists, for he appears only when he is listed with or next to her mother. Triangulation is a particular way of organizing time and space during differentiation. Here her father takes Eric's place beside her mother, maintaining a kind of oedipal triangle where there is always a couple and Hannah, so that she is never alone with either parent. But in this new textual family Hannah is also no longer trapped within a triangle between her mother and her father. Instead, her mother and father's respective bodies are in two separate but parallel columns labeled "mum" and "dad," and Hannah's body is on the left margin of the page. Hannah's body here is represented by a list of the ways Hannah's parents influenced her personal values and achievements, and her body is spatially separate from their bodies. Here there are the beginnings of cause and effect, linking her parents' respective behaviors and values with her own.

Similarly, her lists representing her relationship with Eric create two separate but parallel bodies (see Table 4). This list is transformative of her relationship with Eric as well as of how she is using the lists themselves. She describes what she wants out of a separation from Eric, which includes her need to locate her self. In this list, where she is locating her self, she notes the need to locate her self further, and this level of locating consists of becoming more of who she wants to be: more caring for both herself and the world around her.

This list illustrates the newly found complexity in the exploration process. She is not merely holding up a mirror to see herself, she is simultaneously locating and creating herself, and not exclusively in relationships. She is creating new possibilities for herself within the space between the inner psychic reality and the external world, and, in the process, creating the connection between herself and others; that is, she has created and is using transitional space.[√] She is creating her own texted, embodied subjectivity within her lists.

TABLE 3 The Oedipal Triangle

Hannah	Mum	Dad
personal credo	sake for want learn new skills	liberal
values	work hard keep busy be productive save money nature	education arts perfectionist tidy/organized be successful
primary achieve	have child ambition thru her	provide for family
disappointment	lack of degree creativity only hobby	death after retire
missing element	closeness post Hannah marriage inner conflict	adult relationship generation gap
how h/she wounded me and taught	temper fear unpredictable (please people late develop and look to self	aloof and absent too old
inspired me	therapy, inner mother	therapy inner father
gift to me	love/strength skills/values money	love skills/values money

Table 4 Separating from Eric

Eric's needs	Hannah's needs
strong marriage	content with self
feel loved	continual growth
needed	educational growth
important	self reliance
to be given affection	independence
feel am proud of me	inner happiness
speak of me	time with friends
feel can make H. happy	possibly children
feel trusted	improve health
can explore children idea	less preocc. with body
	enjoy sex/love
E.'s life goals	H.'s life goals
useful job/contribution	travel
good career prospects	charity work
needed at work	care of environment
part of work altruistic	care of diet
	vegi/[?]
	enjoy free time
	more accepting
	less perfectionist
	religious anchor
	feel useful life

This subjectivity is no longer merely a collection of abusive behaviors. Instead, Hannah has begun to create a list of temporally linked experiences enumerating Eric's and then her own desires for the separation. Here she and Eric have not only different bodies but also differently desiring bodies. This transformation is remarkable. As Hannah creates the differentiated bodies of her parents and Eric, she is able to create a space within which her own body can safely come into being; it does so by being imbued with arousal and expectation, the beginnings of embodied time. Hannah's capacities for embodied subjectivity come into being beside not between, her parents' and side by side with, not within, Eric's. She creates one relationship at a time, and bodies within relationships are literally separated by the creation of space on a page. It is at this point, as she comes into being within the diaries, that Hannah attempts suicide for the third time and she and Eric literally separate by getting a divorce.

As the diaries progress, Hannah's body grows. When she first appeared, she was thin, taut, an anorexic list of one-word descriptors narrowly running down the page (see Table 5). The list stands out like an island surrounded by space, creating a feeling of emotional, physical, and experiential deprivation. As the diaries move along, Hannah's body widens, becoming multiple lines of phrases taking up more than half a diary page in width. Nowhere is this process of creating herself more stunning than in a list she creates exploring the "13 key areas of my life." These 13 areas are arranged in order of importance: 1) her marriage, 2) Eric's family, 3) Judaism, 4) her job, 5) her synagogue commitments, 6) friends, 7) her image, 8) her interests, 9) values, 10) pleasures, 11) food, 12) her childhood and 13) her parents. *[Hannah: see parallel to (circle drawn) now also came to 13 (made 12!)]*[2] Because this time her experienced and experiencing self fills an entire diary book, it cannot be reproduced here. This list is complicated,

[2] At the time of our collaboration, Hannah, not remembering this previous list from the diaries, had just created a new list of the "13 key areas of her life." The new list is not linear but circular. It will be discussed in the Epilogue, describing the impact of the research on Hannah.

expansive, and at times even messy. It beautifully demonstrates the malleability of her use of lists, for as Hannah explores each of the "13 key areas," she is able to flow from prose, to lists, to prose again, within the containing space of one overarching list. This list tells the story of her life and is where I was able to first piece her together as a whole person. After this list, one line is no longer enough to contain her self, and her bodied lists become filled with potential life and motion.

Simultaneously, the bodies of her parents and Eric become narrow columns of single words running down the page. Her body expands while they are tightly contained in narrow spaces, patrolled and encased within a thick, unyielding membrane of particularly rigid lists. As she begins simultaneously to extricate and create her self by unraveling the enmeshed weaving of her childhood and marriage, her parents and her ex-husband are safely nailed to the page. And she, for the first time, has freedom of movement within the lists.

Creating an experience of bodies is risky business for survivors of sexual trauma because the memorial processes required for differentiation comprise embodied interactions from the past, including incidents of abuse. With the lists, Hannah has the ability to monitor space and time, so the bodies conjured up are clearly visible and under her exclusive control. There is a certain amount of space on the page between her body and each of theirs. Thus, she is able to create her body while pulling theirs out of her, barring their access to her. She is able to watch and patrol their boundaries.

The transitional spaces of the diaries enable Hannah to play with textual formats and gradually pull herself out from within other people. She can wrap a membrane around her experiences to create her own externalized, skinned body within the list. Here she creates a visual inner and outer, them and I. Unraveling her childhood abuses from those she experienced as an adult, she creates an embodied, organized memory of her mother and Eric, then her father and mother. She simultaneously creates bodies (space) and time. Doing so within lists ensures that she can emerge, remember, and continue to go on being through time

TABLE 5: Who Is Hannah
But what is the real me?
caring
a good listener
sensitive
easily upset and tearful
a good memory
enjoys children
finds it easy to talk to people
smiles
honest and open
enjoys theatre, arts, culture
assertive with authority
obedient to authority and rules
easily conforms
good eye for colour and design
gets involved
reasonable efficient
punctual
flexible
likes to plan ahead in a job to avoid stress
enthusiastic
alternative to the world around
enjoys travel and new experiences
intellectual and quick mind
not scared of hard work
uncompetitive
not sporty
doesn't like change
difficult making decisions
low self esteem
puts own values, time etc. last
anxious
picks up on other's moods

and space as she is held within her diaries, and her parents and Eric are captured within her lists. She concretizes a leap of faith. Thus, the lists provide a space for perhaps the only relationship within which Hannah can create the capacity for faith in continuity in the face of differentiation.

For instance, in her last diary, Hannah's relationship with a new boyfriend, Mark, is contained exclusively within lists (see Table 6). In the first list introducing and creating his body, he is separated from her not by a large, patrolled space on the page, but first through a signifier of overt contrast "vs.," and then by a colon. These indicate a connecting separation, successful differentiation.

Creating the Capacity for Traumatic Meaning-Making

As discussed, culture shapes temporal linking and meaning-making, limiting the ways in which victims are able to digest abusive experiences. In the diaries, Hannah can gather and organize her experiences through her own way of creatively using multiple layers of language without being flooded with memories of abuse. She does this by creatively altering the structure of her text, breaking each memory down into smaller, more digestible morsels of experience, and often dissecting each within numbered subsections of a list. For instance, when she is exploring the potential roots of her bulimia, she suddenly shifts to a list within which she remembers her father's bulimic behavior and how he pulled her into it by forcing her to finish his meals by threatening to vomit after dinner if she did not eat all his food (see Table 7).

This list has a specific structure, reflecting how Hannah gathers this memory by dividing it into three numbered sections. She begins by listing her father's bulimic behaviors around food (Nos. 1–2). Under No. 2 she collects memories of how her father used his disorder against her by threatening to vomit his food if she did not eat it for him. This second section of the list structurally connects her father's disordered eating to her by indicating how she was reeled in to eat for him as a substitute body. In section No. 3 she remembers how as a child she always threw up after meals. In fact, according to this list, she vomited so often her throat developed sores. In this list, she is creating a space within which to accumulate—to gather and make meaning of—her memories of eating

TABLE 6: Connecting with Mark

Mark vs. Hannah

Catholic vs Jew

family vs no family

few friends vs many friends

seeking commitment: fearing commit

ready to settle down: not wanting

placid: anxious

spontaneous: planned

low pace/energy: high energy

introvert/quiet: extrovert

stable: emotional

acceptant: controlling

go w/flow: manipulates life

nonexperimental: experimental

lo risk activities: high risk

traditional: nontraditional

in her family and her excessive vomiting as a child. She does not directly link her vomiting to being force-fed. Instead, after the list, she switches back to prose to wonder whether his eating in the past is linked to her disordered eating in her present. She seems to use this numbered list as a space to gather her past and then use this past to make potential meaning of her present.

Similarly, she divides another list into sections in order to discuss her anger (see Table 8). In this list, further dividing each section into subsections, she discusses, in addition to her anger, how the nature of her anger differs depending on the person at whom

TABLE 7: Dad and Food

1. Dad always bragged about good manners to leave some food as a sign of satisfaction to host (dad)

   Yet mum made me eat all up (mum)

2. Dad dreamed of a table meal

   couldn't taste food

   didn't enjoy eating

   ate only to survive

   chewed and spat out meat fibre

   made himself sick over the years if overate

   said he'd be sick if ate any more

   gave me his food to finish for him—I felt had to

   brush tongue to vomit sounds

   used glass pole for constipation

3. All my yrs of tonsillitis and appendicitis, I was always sick. ulcerated throat perhaps due to sickness vomiting?

it is directed. She also attempts to compare and contrast her view of her anger with Eric's view of her anger. This list indicates continuing internal development, as Hannah is able to experience a nuanced range of agitated self-states that occur for her in relation to others. Anger is now a broad and meaningful category of experience. In addition, by remarking on Eric's and her own view of her anger, she is continuing to locate and differentiate herself in relation to him.

This list provides a flexible space for the development of intentional meaning, as Hannah explores triggers for feelings and how they change with different people in different relational contexts. She is able to contemplate causes and consequences of emotion

TABLE 8: Hannah and Anger

Q [QUESTION] What Hannah does when angry

with 'official people'
- — assertive
- — seek higher authority
- — stand ground and refuse to be put off
- — tell them what I want them to do
- — tell them how I feel
- — reaction—smug guilt forgotten

with 'incompetent average people
- — show displeasure
- — e.g. overtake/horn lights (car) . . .
- — e.g. swear if necessary shout cry
- — reaction afterwards—tense anxious heartbeat loss of appetite, intense memory for decades, block incident if possible, anger doesn't satisfy. Violent thoughts out of all proportion to incident.

With E's family
- — avoidance
- — plan conversation ahead
- — plan to recount 'good incidents'
- — to ensure approval avoid their anger (offset good vs. bad)
- — diffuse situations and smooth over tensions between others
- — (stop before happens
- — avoid anger between others by leaving room. Get upset
- — avoid sides and strong views where I'd have to defend self and face criticism or disagreement
- — be perfect person
- — if criticized, become submissive, avoid eye contact, apologize, make excuses

with E (E's view)
- — make sarcastic comments
- — talk intentionally quiet
- — stop talking

continued on next page

— say ‘bad idea’ and nothing else
— sulk brood for days and don’t forget
— refer back to incidents days later ‘I told you so’ mentality
— overly logical—hundreds of reasons/angle on why I should get my way
— manipulate in way persuade E to change views e.g. put benefits to E
— hurtful things—out of proportion to incident
— tone of speech and manner change—curt and offhand
— stop eating as punishment—as upsets E.

(Hannah’s view)
— feelings of being trapped
— voice changes to precise and least amount of words and least room for misunderstanding if I’m critical
— block feelings inside myself
— sometimes feel violent and want to throw things, lie on floor and scream

---

and action without fear, a state that is the basis for self-agency (Fonagy and Target, 1998). In both Tables 7 and 8, creating smaller and smaller subsections is a process of chewing up her formerly indigestible experiences into more manageable pieces until she is able to create meaningful temporal links. She does this by creating lists that can be embodied in different ways and with unlimited subsections, within which she can safely link, not equate or dissociate, inner and outer, self and other. The past is now meaningfully linked to the present.

The Importance of Future Planning to Escape the Present

Temporal linking not only creates an escape from the past (Merleau-Ponty, 1962), it is also a leap into the future. Hannah accomplishes this future escape through her creation of plans. Plans for future action seem to be how Hannah self-regulates when she is feeling most out of control. Not surprisingly, then, her plans often involve her body as the site of control. These multiple levels of control also help Hannah regulate her self and others in the face of dissociated material.

In one entry, Hannah describes "sobb[ing] uncontrollably" after sharing a "disturbing" dream in which she cuts off her own genitals. Immediately after writing this, she creates a short, curt list of three things she must do to take control of her body: limiting how often she weighs herself and looks in the mirror; working cognitively on changing her body image; and focusing on altering how she feels when she is in her clothes.

Here her history of abuse is not merely peeking, it is screaming out in her dreams, and she responds with a powerful iron fist. She plans ways to control her body as well as her minded experience of her body. She collapses all capacity for in favor of clinging to her dogma, an eating disorder. She encases herself in external rules that create an illusion of going-on-being. These rules then create temporal links, and there is no space of interaction, thus, no space for accumulation or capacity for. She plans to regulate not only her food intake but also her experience of her body, to control how often she can "see" it (while gazing into the mirror or weighing herself). She organizes a plan to regulate and control her experience of her body.

In this list, Hannah demonstrates the complexity of embodiment. This list is not merely about dieting; Hannah wants to change the way she feels within her body. She wants not to have to look at it, weigh it, or feel its beginnings and endings in contact with clothes. These sensations cannot be changed by losing weight. They are altered only by getting rid of her body entirely, through merging or erasure, and by solidifying her mind through external structures of organization. This example illustrates how easily the profound disembodiment of trauma and eating disorders can be reinforced through the external psychoanalytic organization of mind that often excludes the body.

Her inability to maintain a capacity for, a space from which to create meaning, results in her tightening her skin around her, making herself disappear. It is a desperate and profoundly limited, not a creative, use of language. It represents the only space she can maintain at this point, the only space within which she can create a capacity for faith in going-on-being and from which she may be able to create temporality. The eating-disordered behavior, then, is the faith that gathers her experiences toward a future—"if only I were thinner, smaller, could not feel my boundary," etc. She is creating temporal links by dogmatically controlling her body.

But there is a paradox. Efforts to get rid of her body by losing weight simultaneously erase and locate the body, threaten and cohere the stability of the self. Hannah may wish to get rid of her body and its unlinked experiences of abuse, but she also needs to make sure it is there, for it remains her only space of meaning-making and is the container of her memories of abuse.

Weighing herself and looking in the mirror compulsively are behaviors that measure both the body's absence and its presence. Gazing in the mirror provides a concrete representation of where Hannah is and where she is not. She can know her body as an object gazed on from outside herself. But objectifying the experience of the body sustains the evacuation of embodied experience. Here, one experiences one's body as others might see it, from the outside looking in, not phenomenologically, from within the skin. Thus, her body becomes an image, creating distance between her unlinked memories and the experience of being in her body. In other words, it creates space and probably safety. And by constantly experiencing her body from outside, she is continually creating and watching her skin boundary. Doing so visually creates space between self and other as well as between inside and outside. The gaze may also serve to hold her—being bathed in her own vision of her body might strengthen and shore up her external boundary, her skinned cohesion.

But creating boundaries in this way also depends on her visual memory, as her body experience becomes a vision from outside, not a multidimensional experience from within. Her own body becomes just another character in one of her dissociated movies that she watches from afar. Then the body as image remains unlinked. But this process is a circle, for she cannot possibly create embodied experience without having access to embodied experience, unless she can create a transitional space, neither inner nor outer, within which to represent externally and hold her intolerable experience. The lists become her transitional space. Like her physical body, her listed body becomes enmeshed abusively in others until she extricates it to her list, where it emerges as an anorexic skeleton of deliberate, cautious, unlinked one-word lines. The lines of her text widen as her capacities to gather and link experience deepens.

Clearly, Hannah uses plans to mediate her paradoxical desires to remember to forget her self, a paradox that hints at the great ambivalence and struggle in the creation of temporal continuity. Planning may at once be formative of self-experience and yet cut it off. Plans about planning in particular seem to serve the function of her taking sudden control to foreclose exploration as well as potential fragmentation by binding her self tightly within a list. Here plans come to be meditative, as anxieties that were threatening to surface and overwhelm her fall to the side as she narrows her awareness and concentrates only on the multiple levels of planning. Rituals of lists wind her skin tighter and tighter around her until there is no bodied space that, by its very existence, is an opportunity for memories of invasion or experiences of and spaces for fragmentation. She binds herself in the present by planning for the future.

By planning she can also make spatial transitions within the diary. For example, when she is leaving for the eight-week business trip referred to earlier, she feels so out of control that she shoplifts a watch from an airport shop. She creates a list planning how much she is "allowed" to eat. She then explores where she is "currently" by creating a list of her recent achievements. Next she creates a list planning what she will do when she returns from her trip eight weeks later.

She first attempts to control and cohere her body by planning her food intake. Planning what to eat is also planning what to experience, voiding herself of any intolerable experience both in the moment of writing the plan and in the future when she will be implementing the plan. She is tightly controlling her going-on-being by planning for what will be experienced internally and externally and limiting what she will ingest. She then locates her competent self through a list of work and personal achievements and integrates these aspects of herself within one list. Finally she takes control over her self-experience in the moment by launching herself through time to what she will do when she returns from the trip.

Here she manages her newly created experience of anticipation and expectation by effectively erasing the anxiety-provoking trip while sitting in the airport. Traveling within her text, she is able to hold herself together and create continuity throughout the spatial changes, providing temporal stability. But exercising this temporal control also propels her into the future away from the present, which then becomes the past, enabling her to regulate the anxiety she experiences in the moment. *[Hannah: avoiding present still plagued by past, dreams of future present is so dissociated it doesn't exist can only assess "present" in past—i.e. when can see at a distance]*[3]

Without the ability to flee textually from her anxiety and memories, Hannah might be forced to dissociate even more of her awareness or rely on aggressive control and destruction of her own "real" body for coherence. But with lists to plan during such moments of potential fragmentation, Hannah is able to tighten the boundary and holding of the transitional space and make it thick and seemingly impenetrable. Within this fortress, Hannah can begin to expand her linking. She can lessen her use of and reliance on dissociation and self-destruction to create and use a future. *[Hannah: list is an adult activity creativity (art) is childlike]*[4]

---

[3] Hannah noted that she still avoids experiencing her present by dreaming or planning for the future. She said she dissociates her present experience so that it can exist only as a past when she assesses it and can experience it at a distance.

[4] Hannah remarked that she felt the lists were an example of "adult" behavior. She juxtaposed the adult lists with her art and painting, which she believed were more childlike. Her comparison suggests continuing splitting of adult–child (mind–body) experiences. However, as she showed me her current lists, it was apparent that she was beginning to use color and some illustration, externally reflecting continuing internal integration.

Regulating Contact by Creating Time/Creating Time by Regulating Contact

The diaries also allow Hannah to hold on to and negotiate her contact with her therapists through her lists of session summaries, which play with the therapeutic "frame." First, she writes summaries of what occurred. Then she adds thoughts she has about the topic of the session and often does not conclude until she has developed a plan of action to address it. For instance, Hannah creates a list summarizing a session in which she discussed what she needs to do to be discharged from the hospital. She creates a second list linking what she learned from the session with what she knows about her relationship to Eric. She concludes with a third list, exploring what might occur to the relationship if she were to change in the ways discussed in the session summary. She does not end the session when she walks through the office door. She stretches the therapeutic membrane until she herself is done with the session, which, here, is only after she has created three lists temporally linking the ways she wants to change with the potential effects on her relationship.

Sometimes she extends these session lists into a planning list of what she should discuss in the next session. As she "ends" one session she begins the next. She plays with time in a way that allows her to regulate her relational contact with therapists. Not only does she stretch the therapeutic space of the previous session by enclosing herself for a longer period of time, she reaches for the membrane binding the future session and physically joins them. She creates a future by controlling and playing with her own and her therapist's continuity, which enables her to be held therapeutically through time by erasing the space between.

Because traumatic responses are easily triggered by intense relationships like therapy (Fonagy and Target, 1998), both closeness with and separation from the therapist can be intolerable. In these lists, an ending and a beginning can be concretely represented on a page, but because in "measured" time there may not be much of a break between her writing about the ending of the session and her beginning to write about the next, these boundaries need not be experienced as depriving, devastating, or disruptive. Hannah is able to moderate the "agonizing sense of the infinite" (Grotstein, 1993) by creating a sense of boundaried, visual continuity. She can symbolically wrap herself tightly or loosely within the therapeutic membrane whenever and however she needs. And by creating this safe continuity, the lists provide the space for her to hold the session in order to make links.

Containing the therapy interactions within the diary also holds them stable so that they do not change from moment to moment. For instance, because her parents and Eric are held rigidly in her lists as abusers, they cannot charm her into collapsing the safe space between them. Similarly, her therapist will remain as Hannah wrote her within the lists, a benevolent helper. She will not move, explode, or attack in the lists. Each time she opens the diaries, she will be exactly where Hannah left her. Hannah is able to hold on to her therapist as an unchanged, stable person in the diaries. Thus it is safe for Hannah to accumulate experience and to take the leap of faith in going-on-being within the therapeutic relationship.

And when sessions are particularly difficult, Hannah is able to use the lists to modify her experiences in order to hold and digest the content of her sessions. For instance, Hannah summarizes a session dealing with how she loses herself in her "unexplained indirect anger" by creating a numbered list of her therapist's comments. She translated Nos. 4 and 5 on this list into diagrams (see Table 9).

Here she transforms anxiety-provoking, abstract material of a session into discrete numbered, written points. She then translates these words into diagrams, providing yet another form to hold her experience and further demonstrating the flexibility of the creative use of language and symbolization within her transitional spaces. She is able to shift from prose to lists and from lists to diagrams in her attempts to try to temporalize her experience and be able to take in her therapist's comments. Here Hannah is able to create a context where she can play with ideas in her own way to begin to experience them as ideas (Fonagy and Target, 1998). This is key. As Fonagy and Target note, "for the abused

TABLE 9: Translating Sessions

1. loose self—what I need/want?
2. blame of other— . . . not seeing circular causality but linear
3. unexplained indirect anger

4–5.

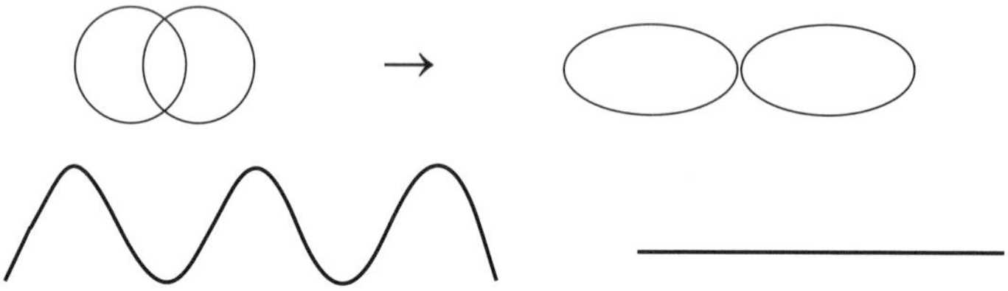

child, the adult's mental world is too real a threat to permit play and is thus shunned and avoided" (p. 107). In the lists, Hannah is able to create her own spaces within which to safely hold and organize her therapist's thoughts, and, through them, she is able to create her own feelings and ideas. Within the transitional spaces of her lists, she is able to recreate a safe version of finding herself in her mother's and therapist's mind and body by holding both in her text.

Accumulations

> The category of mastery is irrelevant to the kind of self–other awareness at stake in the moment of faith, where all that exists of importance is the fact that we are real together, living in the amazing sense of becoming more and more real, where destructiveness makes love real, and love makes destructiveness creative (Eigen, 1981, p. 416).

It is extremely challenging to hold the complexities of temporality when dealing with trauma, but this capacity is absolutely necessary for healing. As Eigen writes, having faith in a "real" connection makes life creative, but if most of your relationships have involved invasion, treachery, and abuse, there can be no "real" faith. Thus, nothing can be "for real." This complexity of faith is why I marvel at Hannah's use of lists.

Certainly Hannah's diaries functioned as transitional space within which she was able to house and make meaning of experience. But this form of holding alone could not create this faith. She had to evolve her own way to "use" these experiences, which in the diaries meant playing with the structure of her text. This structural play, creating visual boundaries for herself and others, enables her to regulate relational access and contact and thus lessens traumatic repetition within the diaries. Through this process, Hannah creates the capacity for faith in space and time. In so doing, she demonstrates that Winnicott's (1970, 1971) limiting membrane, the psychic skin that holds the integrated psyche–soma, separating inner from outer, self from other, is actually spatialized, embodied time.

The process of healing that Hannah creates for herself is a lyrical and structural improvisation occuring as she moves within the diaries from prose, to lists, to diagrams, and back again. Just as music is created by intervals, the bounded spaces in between notes, it is in the movement between different textual structures that Hannah creates temporal linking, meaning-making, her own subjectivity. She speaks what is unspeakable in the motion of her text, where the multiplicity of her experiences can be accumulated not dissociated.

Given the formative functions of her lists, it may come as no surprise that, as she begins to create temporalized bodies of lists, she also reduces her bulimic activity until, by the last diary, she is no longer bingeing and purging, and the text is almost exclusively composed of lists. *[Hannah: they're still compulsive].*[5] It could be said that her lists merely took over Eric's function as the regulator of her experience. After all, she had used Eric as the container for years during which she was not always actively bulimic. Once she was separated from him, her lists increased dramatically, perhaps indicating that she was substituting them for Eric.

---

[5] Hannah felt that her lists were a compulsive substitute for bulimia.

Furthermore her lists at that point are culled mostly from her interactions with the Celestine Prophesy (Redfield, 1993). In other words, it is not only that Hannah may be using the lists to substitute for her bulimic symptoms, but that they are lists created under the rubric of an ideological parent figure. Being held within an ideological, parental membrane may have contributed to her no longer bingeing and purging. Such a setup would indicate not necessarily healing through self-reflection and the creation of time, but better management of her symptoms through yet another merged relationship with an omnipotent parent. *[√]*

There is no question that the compulsion of list-making was substituted for that of bulimia and self-mutilation, but in many ways, the lists also facilitate her healing in profound ways. Although both bulimia and her lists function to externalize her anxieties, bulimia is a complex contradiction of self-destruction in the service of survival that enables the perpetuation of "unspoken" and unheard abusive relationships. This survival requires using the female body as a form of currency toward psychic unity; thus, it is a process of survival that plays into the cultural dynamics of sexual abuse, requiring a further objectification and sacrifice of the (female) body. In the lists, however, Hannah developed her own "transgressive spaces" (Alcoff and Gray, 1993) where her body could be created and held, not sacrificed, as she attempted to manage and integrate her self-experiences on her own terms.

While she continued to externalize her experience, she was not flushing it down the toilet. Instead she accumulated experiences on the page, moving from acting out the abuse within herself, to attempting to hold it outside herself. As she did this, she created a temporal linking process that was in between spaces of repeating and remembering, and under her exclusive control. She was able to "see" her experiences ordered in time and space, creating links of cause and effect and continuity, so that abuse no longer "just happened."

Perhaps the most important and unique function of the lists was their potential for Hannah to revisit and thus rework her traumatic experiences. With bulimia she was, as Davies and Frawley (1992, 1994) have termed, the abuser, victim, and rescuer. In the lists, however, the original abusers played their respective roles, and she erased or moderated her presence and absence. As Alcoff and Gray (1993) note, singling out the survivor for therapy locates the problem within her, as it is she who repeats instead of remembers, which, as described earlier, serves to retraumatize. Similarly, dissociation as a model of trauma, while bringing to light many effects of trauma, also locates the problem in the victim, while keeping the perpetrator safely in the past and having no links to a patriarchal social system that condones and disavows a continum of male violence against women and children (Alcoff and Gray, 1993; Rice, 1996; Haaken, 1998). After all, a survivor "repeats" abusive experiences with someone else; therefore, the problem is not that she repeats but that people are willing to act abusively toward her, while others are willing to ignore it or blame her for the abuse.

Holding her abusers' bodies within the text provided a space for their culpability, so that Hannah's experiences of abuse were no longer privatized within her mind and body. She did not have to resort to creating meaning only by erroneously taking control through self-blame and self-destruction. She developed agency—a potential future—through her own form of justice, transforming paralyzing, trauma-induced helplessness. Doing so not only allowed her to make meaning of her abuse in a transformative way, it also enabled her to create links between her parents' and Eric's respective treatment of her and their own stories of traumatic experiences by providing them with memory and a limited form of subjectivity.

For instance, in the diaries, Hannah described regularly waking to her mother screaming in the middle of the night. In her final list about her mother, she notes that her mother was one of the children transported from London to live in the countryside during the Blitz. Her mother had repetitive nightmares that she was sleeping back in the foster home, and a man walked into her room and approached her bed. At this point, she would wake up screaming. During one of our collaborative meetings, Hannah and I simultaneously wondered aloud about her mother's history of abuse. Hannah then proceeded to pull together previously chaotic snippets of her mother's abusive behaviors into a less confusing story. Her mother's being abusive as a way of dealing with her own history seemed to lift the responsibility from Hannah's shoulders.

Although speculation is far from certainty, it seems that some trauma festered within her mother's relationships. As Fonagy and Target (1996) and Bion (1962) note, unthinkable thoughts cannot be digested or metabolized and thus are passed from one generation to the next. Trauma, then, is held and recreated within the relational space, the space from which the capacity for temporal linking emerges, disrupting development transgenerationally. We can only hope that Hannah's use of her diaries as a space within which consciously to embody these unthinkable thoughts has disrupted such intergenerational transmission. "In the daylight of analysis the ghosts of the unconscious are laid and led to rest as ancestors whose power is taken over and transformed into the newer intensity of present life, of the secondary process and contemporary objects" (Loewald, quoted in Mitchell, 1998, p. 850).

Hannah's lists enable her to lay her ancestral ghosts to rest by linking them to herself in her past and to their own respective pasts and cultural moments. Creating time is a cultural and individual phenomenon, enabling and requiring that each body be embedded within a particular cultural context and temporally linking the social and the psychological with intention and activity. This linking of the social and the psychological, reflection with action, is absolutely key to any kind of transformation (Freire, 1972), and it is achieved only through the "fullness" of embodied time (Tutu, quoted in Tronto, 2003, p. 123).

Epilogue

Tidying Up the Story

And I am not alone
while my love is near me
I know it will be so
Until it's time to go
So come the storms of winter
And then the birds in spring again
I do not fear the time

—Sandy Denny, "Who Knows Where the Time Goes?"

No life can be conveyed accurately within the linear space of a book. Even though this book is based on Hannah's life as it was represented within her own books, her diaries did not squeeze her life into a two-dimensional space. Her text was chaotic, bursting at the seams, and the structure of her narrative became three-dimensional and at times appeared to be in motion. I know as a reader that this structure was discomforting and confusing, so, in writing this book, I tried to strike a balance between conveying this life of her text and presenting the integral components and important analytic turns in a digestible form.

The act of translating Hannah's life into my own feminist psychoanalytic language was a form of invasion, whether this was done collaboratively or not. Indeed, Stacey's (1988) words keep echoing in my head because she is correct—collaboration is not a substitute for analyzing power relationships. But what do you do when your collaborator does not collaborate the way you expect but makes the analysis of these power dynamics quite difficult? As this circular question hints, collaborating with Hannah required my letting go of my expectations for not only the level of collaboration, but also that of negotiation. Without a space for negotiation, it is difficult to productively and creatively address power and other relational dynamics (Pizer, 1998; Slavin and Kriegman, 1998).

For instance, as I mentioned in the first chapter, we had scheduled a week of meetings during which time Hannah would read my analysis, respond within the text and we would discuss this process in person. Her comments about this process would form part of this chapter. As the week neared, however, Hannah began filling it with work commitments. As our meetings came and went, she had not found the time to read the analysis. In other words, we were stuck in a power struggle for which we had a very limited time to negotiate. In the end, I had to find a way to let Hannah change our level of collaboration as she needed. Doing so meant not actually collaborating at the level I had planned.

I found Hannah's various forms of resistance heroic and fascinating when I was writing about them. Having her resist me in the moment of our collaboration, however, was another story. Despite "knowing" her as I did at that point, I was surprised that the Hannah I was creating in my text was the Hannah I was collaborating with. Hannah resisted those who attempted to annex her for their own gain. Even though we had embarked on this collaboration together, we never created the necessary space to go "head to head" (Bromberg, quoted by Pizer, 1998). Instead, we went body to body, so to speak, resisting and struggling in the unspoken spaces of enactments: she filling her time with things other than the collaboration, and I talking myself into believing that this was what she needed to do to titrate her contact with the analysis. So this collaboration created the typical dynamics of a clinical analytic relationship, but without the time necessary to negotiate them.

In the end, Hannah did read the analysis. She was engrossed by it. Then she reread her diaries. She did not, however, comment on the process and "talk back" against my analysis in the way I had planned. Her comments in the text were primarily clarifications and agreements. She made the most active comments in the adolescent diaries, where she connected my observations about friendship patterns to what was going on in her family at that time. She filled in some of the experiences absented from her diary text, for instance, letting me know that her adolescent dieting was not as much fun as she had represented in her diary. She said that reading the analysis of her adolescence was the most difficult emotionally, as she was filling in the blanks with the trauma that was really going on. The frequency of her comments in these chapters indicates that she was quite engaged with it.

Her interactions with the analysis of the adult diaries, on the other hand, were sparse. These focused, again, on clarifying details, tying observations I made about her relationship to Eric with that of her mother (as in her diaries, her father was fairly absent in her comments) and agreeing with the analyses of how she projected her aggression onto Eric and her abusive relationship with her body. Although she said the analysis of her adult diaries was much easier for her to read, she made fewer comments, and, during our collaborative meetings, it seemed more difficult for her to discuss them. Instead, she kept pulling our discussion into the present. She described the growth she had experienced since writing these diaries. Her assertion makes me wonder if she was able to hold her discomfort about the analysis of her adult diaries and if she was actually connecting with them deeply on a different, unspeakable level.

Similarly, when discussing her experience of the collaboration itself, she instead presented her own verbal list of the ways she had transformed herself during the three years I had been analyzing her diaries. This list does contextualize the analysis of her diaries, but in a different way than I expected. As I found in the analysis, Hannah creates her temporal links, her time and space, in externalized, ordered spaces she can see and manipulate. Therefore, she really could not talk back against or with my analysis, because doing so required an internal space from which to create meaningful links. Instead of commenting on the process (or on her more recent adult diaries), she enacted my analysis by creating lists: one verbal and one on paper.

Tidying up the Analysis—The Unique Function of Diaries

You will recall that the diaries provide the paradoxical transitional phenomena that Winnicott (1971) described as being integral to development, because they function as being neither self nor other, inner nor outer. They are concretely physical—they are words organized on a page. Hannah can hold and touch them. They are real and they are out there. But they are also illusory and inside. They have inner symbolic meanings and a wealth of fantasized intentions that are beyond physical reality. They exist in both spaces simultaneously and seem to create a bridge for Hannah between multiple spaces of existence and dissociated self-states.

By concretizing fantasy and reality, inner and outer, the diaries allow for playing, exploring possibilities, without being too fantastical to be unreal but not so real as to be frightening or overwhelming. And, again, being in a malleable text, Hannah is in control; she can regulate and titrate what she can handle. She can structure the text to wrap tightly around her as a protective skin when she recalls abusive incidents in a list, or she can loosen the grip when remembering less traumatic moments in prose.

But, in order for Hannah to use the diaries as transitional objects, she must allow herself to "exist neither in reality nor in fantasy, but in a potential space between the two" (Ogden, 1992, p. 620). Becoming an experiencing subject requires actually traveling in the space between fantasy and reality within which "symbols are created and imaginative psychological activity takes place" (p. 622). It is within this paradoxical space that a person comes to feel alive, to experience, and to have a subjectivity. For survivors of trauma, though, such a space can be terrifying in its uncertainty. Stability is tremendously important for a survivor, who often seeks "an antidote to her painful awareness of inconsistencies that plague both herself and those with whom she is involved" (Layton, 1998, p. 132). So the very process necessary for development and healing is also one that may be most difficult and threatening for a trauma survivor.

The creative ingenuity of the diaries is that they provide a comforting sense of consistency and stability while simultaneously providing a format within which Hannah can challenge this consistency through improvisation. Being entirely under her control, the diaries can function as the holding space between fantasy and reality without dipping into retraumatization. Here she is literally able to play out the process of differentiation by creating temporal bodies in her text. Aron (1996), Mitchell (1997), and Bromberg (1998, 2001), to name only a few, advocate creating multiple shifting meanings; but when one is dealing with analyses involving traumatic memories, this shifting can be experienced as intolerable and can reproduce the already too pervasive sense of unreality and fragmentation that comes with having no sense of going-on-being or of one's self in and of the world. Additionally, there is a narrow, socially patrolled range for potential ways of cohesively going-on-being for all women within a patriarchal culture. Diaries can bridge these contradictory positions and needs.

Bulimia as Resistance

This analysis of Hannah's diaries has allowed me the invaluable opportunity to trace the path of bulimia through her life. With a history of embodied and psychic invasions, Hannah was primed to develop a symptom that would express the distress of being pried open and entered against her will. Here expression found its frame in the culturally "appropriate" behavior of dieting for two adolescent friends and developed into a necessary and valuable way to deal with traumatic experience. That her friendship with Karen culminated in Hannah's stating they were "too close" and led into her disordered eating patterns indicates that her chumship with Karen threatened to bring forth memories and experiences of trauma. Keeping these traumatic memories out of her awareness required not only eliminating Karen as a chum, but also starving, bingeing, and vomiting to excise her female body.

Hannah's diaries also provided phenomenological details of the importance of vomiting and bingeing as two distinct behaviors that evolved over time. While they may often be temporally linked, they are not causally linked. Hannah did not vomit because she binged, she usually binged so she could have the opportunity to vomit. She needed to eject things explosively, violently, and self-destructively from her body. She needed to see and control inside and out. This is very important. And this pattern shifted once she had separated from Eric when the bingeing, filling herself up with food, became paramount, and she often did not even bother to vomit.

As is typical, Hannah's bulimia was merely one of the many destructive and impulsive behaviors with which she was struggling. Although I did not focus on them, she also shoplifted, compulsively masturbated, and obsessively organized and reorganized her wardrobe. She often went on expensive shopping "binges" for the right clothes that would externally alter her internal experiences. Bulimia was one symptom with many facets.

Such an in-depth analysis of bulimia also indicates that, without question, bulimia is a necessary coping behavior staving off potential fragmentation related to trauma. This trauma can be the experience of overt childhood sexual abuse or as Rice (1996) implies, the trauma of growing up within a patriarchy. It is also a complex, brilliant form of resistance taken by silenced people to express silenced traumas that remain in the silenced female body, which refuses to remain docile. After all, "what goes on without saying and what cannot be said for lack of an available discourse, represents the dividing line between the most radical form of misrecognition and the awakening of political consciousness" (Bourdieu, 1977, p. 170). Thus, bulimia can be seen as a struggle to awaken a political consciousness, to create a "transgressive space" (Alcoff and Grey, 1993) within which to express trauma and oppression. However, this consciousness is very difficult to potentiate clinically.

First, bulimia and other eating problems are entrenched, difficult to treat, and massively self-destructive and alienating. To make matters worse, the destructive behaviors are continually rewarded by the misogynist, thin-obsessed culture. Second, to treat bulimia and other eating disorders as a form of potential political awakening could be seen as foisting a therapeutic agenda on the patient. I will say, though, that *any* therapeutic stance foists an agenda on the patient. This particular stance is prominent because it challenges a central tenet of a patriarchy and asks psychotherapy to see the presence of politics in each treatment and each theoretical stance.

Finally, the form of treatment requires that the clinician watch the patient walk the very thin line between life and death, with no guarantees. This danger does not put into question forced hospitalizations and forced feedings across the board, but it does require real exploration of the psychotherapist's need to destroy the patient's expressions that have become so desperate as to be self-endangering. This is easier said in a book about a diary written by someone who I know survived than it is in real life working with uncertainty and life-and-death issues. But knowing that so few women with eating disorders actually "recover" and that, even if they do, the Western female gender role actually requires a subthreshold eating disorder, it seems that the way we treat these disorders, and women in general, must change. Observing the function of this behavioral phenomenon from a cultural and intrapsychic perspective is the only way to begin to understand the paradox of bulimia as a necessary form of temporal linking for individual women as well as for the cultural body.

Trauma and Healing

While the collaboration between Hannah and me just barely tapped into the profound effects of trauma, it did make clear that these effects are still omnipresent in every interpersonal interaction for Hannah. As McLane (1996) states, trauma is hidden in the very bodied spaces our culture tends to disavow and discredit. Here Hannah's body appears in the spaces of disavowed experience, textual shifts, and intersubjective expectations for subjectivities.

With no body, no sense of temporal continuity, Hannah was at the mercy of an abusive environment. Eric and other men had the authority not only to tell her who she is and what she wants, but also to define the symbolic ranges of her experiences. Of course, these heterosexual relationships mirrored her parental relationship in which she was an absent subject and emerged as a present object for abuse, control, and invasion. These abusive relationships were also supported by a culture that identifies women as the property of men.

Her experiences of trauma were mirrored and reinforced by so many interactions with men who were repeatedly invasive and abusive that Hannah's process of dissociation in response to these and previous experiences of sexual abuse became her discourse of her female desire. Here the cultural narration of an absent female discourse of desire (Fine, 1988) became a female discourse of absent desire through her dissociative responses to sexual trauma. The cultural tendency to blame the victim was then reinscribed by normalizing this traumatized absence of experiencing and desiring. This absence became more dangerous because it left Hannah open to more abusive experiences with men as she was unable to name or experience these interactions as abuse and thus found it difficult to stop them. She became dependent on a phallocentric discourse of desire and victim-blaming to create and shape her own desire. This desire-shaping discourse was also heterosexist, as relationships with women were neutered of their sexual content and, in the adult diaries, practically banished from her text in favor of writing about relationships with men.

Without the necessary foundation for Hannah to experience her experiences, bulimia seemed to provide an invaluable service of temporalizing her experience and creating a sense of going-on-being. The constellation of symptoms—"holding" the numbers of her weight, tracking food, and planning diets—became her temporal links. Unfortunately, bulimia also functioned to "hold" her at a level of repeating and not remembering her traumas.

Hannah's creation of the malleable transitional spaces within the diaries themselves was one of the most significant steps toward her beginning to experience her experience and remember her past. Using lists and other textual structures helped her vomit out her experiences on paper, instead of into the toilet, and provide a permanent location of holding for these externalized experiences. It also provided the space for the capacity to create temporal links, to symbolize and regulate her experiences. This space is what most likely allowed her to stop bingeing and purging and provided the safety necessary for her to begin remembering and to integrate dissociated experiences.

The diaries illuminate that the key to healing and transformation is to create the rules of what is speakable for both bodies and minds, knowing that they are inseparable and that they feed each other with meaning. In doing so, Hannah created the capacity to experience, to desire, to fill the absent spaces on her own terms. The diaries enable Hannah to have more of a say in the creation of her temporal links.

Hannah: About Her Transformation and Healing

Before we had a chance to sit down to begin the first meeting, Hannah fell into an excited, fast-paced monologue about time.

> Time's quite important I think. Time's an important concept for me in my life, actually more than just quite. . . . It's a way of structuring my experiences, a way of giving structure to my experiences, because feelings are very confusing and unstructured for me. So a timeline and some sort of literally a linear patterning of before during and after gives me a list, a structured format for what are really confusing, what are unstructured experiences.

She saw time as the most important factor in her healing. Her description of her use of time fits my analysis. For her, however, meaning was limited to that which can be generated chronologically. She was not exactly embracing her experience in time; she was ordering it. This is not the ideal creation of temporal links that are plumped with embodied meaning, but it is not bingeing and purging either.

After discussing time, she proceeded to narrate a list of what she called her recent insights. As she did so, I had the surreal feeling that somehow she had read my analysis even though she had yet to see it. This list is in my own words, paraphrased from the verbal list she rattled off.

1. The importance of time and the need to represent it externally on paper.
2. The role of *The Celestine Prophesy* (Redfield, 1993) and religion as a containing boundary to make meaning of actions.
3. The use of lists to externalize her thoughts.
4. The role of self-inflicted pain to locate her self.
5. The function of bulimia to externalize her experiences.
6. The need for her to project her feelings onto other people by using her relationships to express parts of her self.

To say the content of her list supported my analysis would be an understatement, for she practically outlined it within the first 15 minutes of our initial meeting. She ended this list by saying that being the subject of this analysis had "provided the hooks to hang these experiences on. To put them together."

It seemed that all my care in writing the analysis for her to read was somewhat misspent, for what had the greatest impact was my sustained attention. Ogden (1992) notes that, for Winnicott, it is the recognition that the other is experiencing you as a subject that creates "conditions for a new way of being aware of one's own subjectivity, and subjectivity itself is thereby altered" (p. 622). Within the space of acknowledging my recognition of her as a subject, Hannah was able to experience herself as a subject, or, as she liked to put it, as "an interesting case study."

Sheldrake's (1990) idea of morphic resonance also fits right in here as it describes the function of the space between. He describes a vibrational, connecting morphic field existing between all living things. In this field, one person doing the Sunday crossword puzzles successfully can make it easier for the next. Seen in this way, my analysis of Hannah's diaries may have paved the psychic path for her to integrate more experiences for herself, or her work on her life may have paved my analytic path.

According to Hannah, the second most important component of her healing was her use of lists. Evidently, after she finished keeping a formal diary, she continued to create lists. Her lists now are on paper, on poster board, sometimes painted and in color, and they integrate drawings and nonlinear forms. For instance, her most recent list was called "the 13 key areas of my life!" (see Figure 1).

FIGURE 1: 13 Key Areas of My Life

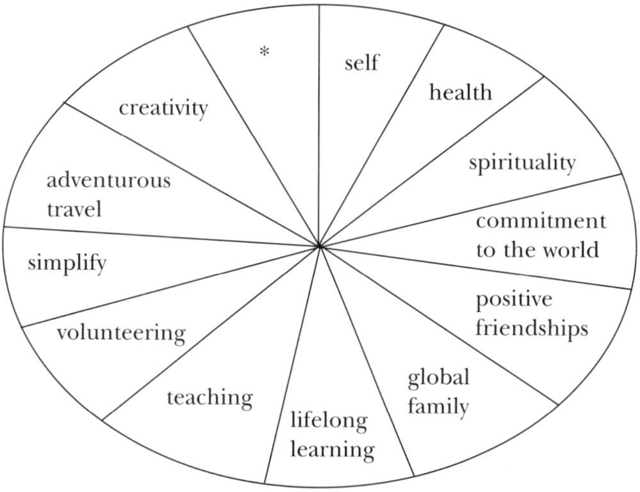

[* Is blank space for future growth.]

Interestingly, the most extensive list in her diaries was also called "the 13 key areas of my life." As I mentioned, this list constituted an entire diary book and alternated exploration lists with explanatory prose. It is fascinating that she created another such list, this time in the form of a wheel. At the time she showed me this list, she had not yet read the adult diaries, and she did not remember their content. I did not mention anything about the similarities to the previous list because I wanted to hear her reaction after she read the diaries, that is, if she thought the similarities were important. And she did think they were important. She was amazed and said she had not remembered making the initial list. She even took the time to create an additional "meta-list" comparing the two lists (see Table 1).

TABLE 1: A Comparison of the Two "13 key areas of my life" Lists

Hospital List	1999 List
marriage	*self
Eric's family	*health
Judaism	*spirituality
job	*commitments to the world
shul/hobbies	positive friendships
friends	global family
image	lifelong learning
interests/hobbies	teaching
values/ideas	volunteering
pleasures	simplify
food/drink	adventurous travel
childhood	creativity
parents	*empty space within which to grow, to create a new key area

* Because it is structured like a wheel, these are the top five key areas.

Not only were the lists different structurally—the new list is a wheel, so it ends where it begins, providing motion and flow—but, as Hannah pointed out, the early lists did not include any mention of her "self" or "health." It was all about Eric and what he wanted, her parents and what they had wanted. Hannah appeared in the earlier list only in her discussion of the foods she enjoyed and the image she wanted to project.

In contrast, the recent list is all about Hannah and her awareness of the world and the activities she does that connect her to that world. She is much more embedded in what she calls a "global family" to which she has a sense of responsibility. Here she is making connections to people as ideas or concepts. She gets to choose her family, volunteer to affect and help her family, but they are also a somewhat amorphous concept. One could say that she is also creating the space to experience her humanness, her place in the world, her interconnectedness and interdependence with others. This is a big step. She has an impact here not only through friendships but also through volunteering and teaching others.

She also has left a space open for potential growth. I see this space as representing her newly found capacity for, her internal space within which she can represent her experience, symbolize it, and transform it, enabling her to conceptualize future growth. Hannah, whose only place of competence and security was work, has developed the ability to "be" (Winnicott, 1971) in more areas of her life.

The third factor contributing to Hannah's healing was her spirituality, culled from *The Celestine Prophesy* (CP) (Redfield, 1993). As she said:

> CP is quite important in terms of there is a life beyond and I can think of it as having had a purpose I came to the earth for and it helps me see why it's been like this . . . and in terms of the shoplifting and things like that it gives me some values about like Karma. . . . It's my own. I've made it my own. . . . That's something Hannah is . . . but it was some creation that I might have a purpose or a link with a higher being, link with a higher self, not just my own higher self but an all seeing being . . . I think I've created boundaries with my imaginary higher self . . . and I have more faith with that relationship than any other with other earth beings. I hadn't said it like that before . . . because I think it's so difficult to differentiate myself from an other in this life. Where do I start and where do they end?

Bingo. Faith + temporal linking = differentiation. Hannah clearly articulates how faith in a higher power enables her to create links that themselves help her differentiate, create boundaries between her self and others as well as about socially appropriate behavior. She creates cause and effect and discusses time as Karma. And, most important, this system is hers. "That's something Hannah is." It is like Winnicott's (1971) transitional object: one cannot ask the child who created it.

It is imperative that Hannah found that system for herself. It is hers, she can take it anywhere, and it helps her create the capacity to organize and contain her self-experience. It helps her create boundaries and provides a structure for making meaning of not only basic things, like interpersonal boundaries and social rules, but also why she is here in this life. It provides Hannah with a sense of effectiveness—for she found it and created her use of the spirituality—while providing a containing sense of membrane-bounded community with social rules within which she does not have to worry about being invaded or invading others. For the first time, she may be experiencing a parental type of relationship with someone or something in which she can create the capacity for faith. She does not have to be parentified or invaded within this relationship.

The importance of spirituality for Hannah did not become clear until our collaborative meetings. In the diaries, she mentions going to church or synagogue, but that seems to take a backseat to other events in her life. During the collaboration, she spoke through a language of "new age" spirituality in the taglines she used and the ways in which she discussed her connection and responsibility to the world.

She told me that, when she was a child, her parents were not religious at all and did not care whether or not she went to church. She described going to church as a way to connect to something. When she married Eric she converted to Judaism as a way of connecting herself to him and his family. When she was returning from her eight-week job in Prague after her divorce, she described arriving in Vienna and searching for a temple, a Jewish welcome center, or a any church, "anything," as she put it, that would be like a "welcoming family to take me in." It was not the theology she required, as evidenced from her willingness to go to a Catholic or Protestant church, or a Jewish welcome center. She needed an externalized omniscient parent to embrace her, shape her so that she could walk through the world.

New-age spirituality enables her to concretize this embrace by looking at the "energy" she puts out and takes in and how all this shapes her interactions. Her spirituality is expansive; it includes her connection to the earth and to other beings in the world, including people and animals.[1] I have described eating disorders as creating a dogmatic frame and a strategy of behaviors within which to walk through the world and make meaning of it while providing a way of engaging with the world. Compared with bulimia, Hannah's version of new-age spirituality is a more flexible and potentially meaningful frame by which to live and engage with the world. She is able to incorporate the frames provided by the *Prophesy* and use them to create her own capacity for. She is able to create meaningful temporal links within this flexible frame.

Hannah in 2005

Throughout the three years of our research, and during the four years since, Hannah created the conditions to continue growing and transforming herself. She mentioned during our meetings that participating in my research helped her claim her voice as a survivor. Shortly after our collaboration, Hannah was interviewed for a magazine article about bulimia. This was the first of many opportunities for her to speak out in a public forum about her experiences. She also became a spokesperson for a national mental health organization working in the area of eating disorders.

---

[1] Along with the dissociation of the centrality of bodies in psychoanalytic theory comes the dissociation of our connection and responsibility to the earth and nonhuman beings. As ecofeminists have pointed out, patriarchies conquer feminine bodies, including the identified "feminine" qualities in men, women's bodies, and the "feminized" bodies of animals and the earth (see Fiddles, 1991; Donovan and Adams, 1996). Just as female bodies are seen as the property of men, the earth and animals are seen as the property of humans. Transgressive spaces, then, must take into account these links if we are to keep traumatic sadistic-masochistic relational dynamics from being displaced onto our relationships with animals, nature, and the earth. These spaces must create meaningful and responsible temporal links—a "real" connection—linking our behaviors as the cause with the effects on animals and the earth.

She worked with this organization to implement research assessing patients' and therapists' respective ideas and experiences of treatment. She asked me to help with this project, and I did. This project instituted an annual eating-disorder conference in London, which Hannah's company organized.

About three years ago, Hannah sold half her consulting business so she could work six months a year and then travel. She split her holiday time between vacationing with tour groups and working as a volunteer for international peace organizations. Now it is not unusual for me to receive postcards from New Zealand, Thailand, or Kuwait: "Greetings from Hannah."

As I was finishing this book, Hannah returned from a three-month volunteer job in the Sudan. She had sold almost all the rest of her business the year before and was in a very strong financial position. She was finishing academic work on a doctoral degree in counseling from an on-line, distance-learning program. She had decided to begin volunteering for an aid organization that works primarily in war zones, and she lobbied for them to send her to Sudan to develop standardized crisis debriefing for the European aid workers. She is not sure whether she will stay in London and volunteer for parts of each year or leave England altogether and take a job directly with the aid agency in Europe. She has described feeling anxious but excited about the width of her life.

I could analyze her choices here and describe her seeking to be surrounded by death, violence, trauma, and hyperstimulation as a repetition. It may be. By Hannah's choosing this form of work, her public and work persona, which has consistently been her space of competence devoid of trauma, is now filled with violence. Furthermore, this public and work persona has now taken over her life, for when she is in the Sudan, even when she is not actually working, she is surrounding by her coworkers and is in her work environment. She is enveloped within a holding skin of her work within her aid organization.

But this continuing attempt to transform a history of trauma can also be seen as her becoming empowered as a person within our global world, a person who identifies and experiences a responsibility to aid others in their struggles. So, again, we have a paradox. The important point is that Hannah, now, is pretty content with her life, her options, and her capacities to choose for herself. Her resistance now is targeted at larger forces and seems much more agentic and effective. As she wrote herself, in response to reading this section about her current life,

- I spend almost all of this rotation coaching others to find their voice, and can only do this as you helped me find mine—thank you!

Hannah describes an important cycle of healing and empowerment that has led her to her current work where she now helps others. If this is a repetition, it certainly is subversive and resistant.

In Closing

While writing this book, I accepted a position as Professor and Women's Center Director at John Jay College of Criminal Justice in New York City. There I integrate clinical work with teaching and research. The clinical work and research both focus primarily on issues of dating, intimate partner and family violence, sexual assault, and eating problems in men and women students. I am immersed in stories of violence much of the day. As in Hannah's diaries, these stories assault, invade, pummel, and at times comfort my body and mind in conscious and unconscious ways. And, as in Hannah's diaries, I struggle with my students as we attempt to make meaning through linking intention and action (temporal links). But, now, as I hear them describe the terror of undifferentiated time and the corresponding use of drugs, food, or violence to hide from this time, only part of me goes with them. And, when I am lucky, I get to see them emerge as they begin to use anticipation (creating a future from a held past) and gradually abandon their self-destructive behaviors as they create new temporal links to make meaning of their abuse.

But I have also seen how easily this growth can turn to retraumatization on different levels of consciousness. I have found that it is imperative to meld feminist theory in the creation of these temporal links, to keep both men and women from reinscribing victim-blaming and other oppressive ideologies in their evolving bodies and minds. Differentiating self-destruction and resistance is integral for healing, but it is extremely tricky in a white, patriarchal culture founded on the control, elimination, disavowal, and destruction of all that is identified as "feminine" and embodied. Thus, transforming trauma necessarily requires exploring how cultural forms of temporal linking (including those which are the foundations of psychotherapy and psychoanalysis) impede and negate healing.

Mohanty (2004) describes mutuality, accountability, and the recognition of common interests as being necessary to create an "active withdrawal of consent and resistance to structures of psychic and social domination" (p. 7). In other words, mutual relationships are only the first step. Resistance can be withdrawn only when systems of domination are acknowledged and disinvested in favor of Eigen's (1981) "real" connection. As he writes, when we are connecting at this level, mastery and domination are not only deconstructed, they cease to be important.

Eigen's description is beautiful in theory, but, when our cultural temporal links creating this connection inscribe oppression and domination, such a connection is quite tricky. Furthermore, the leap of faith necessary to create this "real" connection involves the capacity for temporal linking and differentiation, the very elements that are destroyed by trauma in the first place.

Relational psychoanalytic theory has struggled to create ways of exploring power and privilege within the clinical dyad. But to engage in this process, we also need to create the spaces to explore how political, cultural and social power, and privilege operate within and outside the clinical space. All these levels of analysis are necessary for the creation of the conditions for taking the pivotal leap of faith toward a "real" connection.

Integrating relational psychoanalytic and feminist forms of inquiry creates one potential space within which to take this leap. This was the space I attempted to foster throughout this collaboration but fell short of in a number of areas. After all, implementing this unique alchemy of analyses necessitated holding multiple, contradictory relational positions simultaneously. It required thinking about both of the experiences of us culturally, relationally, and intrapsychically. It required the understanding that where there is power there is also resistance (Foucault, 1972), so when I identified Hannah's acts of resistance as being valuable spaces of her subjectivity I also had to identify the corresponding acts of power and privilege that were working to destroy that subjectivity. These acts included not only Eric's but also my own interactions with Hannah.

Most important, implementing this analysis of Hannah's diaries meant embarking on a vertiginous journey in which familiar forms of temporal linking, time, and space, fell away. And in this fragile, vulnerable state, Hannah and I both had to take a leap of faith that, from the connection we were struggling to create, new ways of being would emerge for both of us. Fortunately, they did.

References

Alcoff, L. & Gray, L. (1993), Survivor discourse: Transgression or recuperation? *Signs: J. Women in Cult. & Soc.*, 18:260–290.

Aron, L. (1996), *A Meeting of Minds: Mutuality in Psychoanalysis.* Hillsdale, NJ: The Analytic Press.

——— & Anderson, F. S., eds. (1998), *Relational Perspectives on the Body.* Hillsdale, NJ: The Analytic Press.

——— & Harris, A. (1993), Sándor Ferenczi: Discovery and rediscovery. In: *The Legacy of Sándor Ferenczi,* ed. L. Aron & A. Harris. Hilldale, NJ: The Analytic Press, pp. 1–36.

Bakhtin, M. M. (1981), *The Dialogic Imagination,* trans. C. Emerson & M. Holquist. Austin: University of Texas Press.

Bateson, M. C. (1989), *Composing a Life: Life as a Work in Progress—The Improvisations of Five Extraordinary Women.* New York: Plume.

Beebe, B., Lachmann, F. & Jaffe, J. (1997), Mother–infant interaction structures and presymbolic self- and object relations. *Psychoanal. Dial.*, 7:133–182.

Behar, R. (1993), *Translated Woman: Crossing the Border with Esperanza's Story.* Boston, MA: Beacon Press.

Benjamin, J. (1995), *Like Subjects, Love Objects.* New Haven, CT: Yale University Press.

Benstock, S. (1988), Authorizing the autobiographical. In: *Feminisms: An Anthology of Literary Theory and Criticism,* ed. R. R. Warhol & D. P. Herndl. New Brunswick, NJ: Rutgers University Press, pp. 1138–1154, 1997.

BjÖerkqvist, K., Lagerspetz, K. M. & Kaukiainen, A. (1992), Do girls manipulate and boys fight? Developmental trends in regard to direct and indirect aggression. *Aggress. Behav.*, 18:117–127.

Bion, W. R. (1959), *Experiences in Groups.* New York: Basic Books.

——— (1962), The psycho-analytic study of thinking. *Internat. J. Psycho-Anal.*, 43:306–310.

Bordo, S. (1993), *Unbearable Weight: Feminism, Western Culture, and the Body.* Berkeley: University of California Press.

Bourdieu, P. (1977), *Outline of a Theory of Practice.* Cambridge: Cambridge University Press.

Bromberg, P. (1998), *Standing in the Spaces: Essays on Clinical Process, Trauma and Dissociation.* Hillsdale, NJ: The Analytic Press.

——— (2001), The gorilla did it: Some thoughts on dissociation, the real and the really real. *Psychoanal. Dial.*, 11:385–404.

Brown, L. M. (1998), *Raising Their Voices: The Politics of Girls' Anger.* Cambridge, MA: Harvard University Press.

——— & Gilligan, C. (1992), *Meeting at the Crossroads.* Cambridge, MA: Harvard University Press.

Bruner, J. (1990), *Acts of Meaning.* Cambridge, MA: Harvard University Press.

——— (1994), Life as narrative. In: *The Need for Story: Cultural Diversity in the Classroom and Community*, ed. A. M. Dyson & C. Genishe. Urbana, IL: National Council of Teachers of English.

Bucci, W. (1997), Symptoms and symbols: A multiple code theory of somatization. *Psychoanal. Inq.*, 17:151–172.

Buechler, S. (1995), Hope as inspiration in psychoanalysis. *Psychoanal. Dial.*, 5:63–74.

Butler, J. (1990), *Gender Trouble.* New York: Routledge.

——— (1993), *Bodies that Matter: On the Discursive Limits of "Sex."* New York: Routledge.

Coetzee, J. M. (1990), *Age of Iron.* New York: Penguin Books.

Collins, P. H. (1990), *Black Feminist Thought: Knowledge, Consciousness, and the Politics of Empowerment.* London: Routledge.

Corrigan, E. G. & Gordon, P. E. (1995), *The Mind Object: Precocity and Pathology of Self-Sufficiency.* London: Karnac Books.

Davies, J. M. & Frawley, M. G. (1992), Dissociative processes and transference countertransference paradigms in the psychoanalytically oriented treatment of adult survivors of childhood sexual abuse. *Psychoanal. Dial.*, 2:5–36.

——— & ——— (1994), *Treating the Adult Survivor of Childhood Sexual Abuse: A Psychoanalytic Perspective.* New York: Basic Books.

de Lauretis, T., ed. (1986), *Feminist Studies/Critical Studies.* Bloomington: Indiana University Press.

Denny, S. (1969), Who knows where the time goes. Fairport Convention, On *Unhalfbricking*, Island Records.

Denzin, N. (1989), *Interpretive Biography.* Newbury Park, CA: Sage.

——— (1992), The many faces of emotionality: Reading *Persona.* In: *Investigating Subjectivity: Research on Lived Experience*, ed. C. Ellis & M. G. Flaherty. Newbury Park, CA: Sage, pp. 17–30.

Dimen, M. (1989), Power, sexuality, and intimacy. In: *Gender/Body/Knowledge/Feminist Reconstructions of Being and Knowing*, ed. A. M.

Jaggar & S. R. Bordo. New Brunswick, NJ: Rutgers University Press, pp. 34–51.
——— (1991), Deconstructing difference: Gender, splitting, and transitional space. *Psychoanal. Dial.*, 1:335–352.
——— (1997), Bodytalk. *Gender & Psychoanal.*, 1:385–402.
——— & Goldner, V., eds. (2002), *Gender in Psychoanalytic Space.* New York: Other Press.
Donovan, J. & Adams, C. J., eds. (1996), *Beyond Animal Rights: A Feminist Caring Ethic for the Treatment of Animals.* New York: Continuum.
Douglas, M. (1966), *Purity and Danger.* New York: Routledge.
——— (1970), *Natural Symbols: Explorations in Cosmology.* London: Routledge, 1996.
Drake, N. (1968), Time has told me, LP, *Five Leaves Left,* Island Records.
Eigen, M. (1981), The area of faith in Winnicott, Lacan and Bion. *Internat. J. Psycho-Anal.*, 62:413–433.
Fabian, J. (1983), *Time and the Other: How Anthropology Makes Its Object.* New York: Columbia University Press.
Ferenczi, S. (1933), Confusion of tongues between adults and the child. In: *Final Contributions to the Problems and Methods of Psycho-Analysis,* ed. M. Balint (trans. E. Mosbacher). London: Karnac Books, 1980, pp. 156–167.
Fiddles, N. (1991), *Meat: A Natural Symbol.* London: Routledge.
Fine, M. (1988), Sexuality, schooling, and adolescent females: The missing discourse of desire. *Harvard Educat. Rev.*, 58:29–52.
——— (1994a), Working the hyphens: Reinventing self and other in qualitative research. In: *Handbook of Qualitative Research,* ed. N. Denzin & Y. Lincoln. Newbury Park, CA: Sage, pp. 70–82.
——— (1994b), Dis-stance and other stances: Negotiations of power inside feminist research. In: *Power and Method: Political Activism and Educational Research,* ed. A. Gitlin. New York: Routledge, pp. 13–35.
——— (1996), Writing the "wrongs" of fieldwork: Confronting our own research/writing dilemmas in urban ethnographies. *Qual. Inq.*, 2:251–274.
Fisher, B. M. (2001), *No Angel in the Classroom: Feminist Pedagogy as Political Practice.* New York: Rowman & Littlefield.
Fiske, J. (1994), Audiencing: Cultural practice and cultural studies. In: *Handbook of Qualitative Research,* ed. N. Denzin & Y. Lincoln. Thousand Oaks, CA: Sage, pp. 189–198.
Flax, J. (1990), *Thinking Fragments: Psychoanalysis, Feminism, and Postmodernism in the Contemporary West.* Berkeley: University of California Press.

——— (1993), *Disputed Subjects: Essays on Psychoanalysis, Politics, and Philosophy.* New York: Routledge.

Fonagy, P & Target, M. (1996), Playing with reality: I. Theory of mind and the normal development of psychic reality. *Internat. J. Psycho-Anal.*, 77:217–233.

——— & ——— (1998), Mentalization and the changing aims of child psychoanalysis. *Psychoanal. Dial.*, 8:87–114.

——— & ——— (2002), Early intervention and the development of self-regulation. *Psychoanal. Psychol.*, 22:307–335.

Foucault, M. (1972), *The Archaeology of Knowledge and the Discourse on Language.* New York: Pantheon Books.

Freedman, N. (1985), The concept of transformation in psychoanalysis. *Psychoanal. Psychol.*, 2:317–339.

Freire, P. (1972), *Pedagogy of the Oppressed,* trans. M. B. Ramos. New York: Herder & Herder.

Freud, S. (1919), "A child is being beaten" A contribution to the study of the origin of sexual perversions. *Standard Edition,* 17:175–204.

Garrett, C. J. (1996), Transformations in time and space: Social theory and recovery from eating disorders. *Eating Disorders,* 4:245–255.

Gentile, K. A. (2000), Healing Through Lyrical Improvisations within the Transitional Spaces of a Diary. Doctoral dissertation, New York University, 2000.

Gergen, K. & Gergen, M. (1993), Narratives of the gendered body in popular autobiography. *Narr. Stud. Lives,* 1:191–218.

Ghent, E. (1990), Masochism, submission, surrender. *Contemp. Psychoanal.*, 26:169–211.

——— (1992), Process and paradox. *Psychoanal. Dial.*, 2:135–159.

Gilligan, C., Lyons, N. P. & Hanmer, T. J., eds. (1990), *Making Connections: The Relational Worlds of Adolescent Girls at Emma Willard School.* Cambridge, MA: Harvard University Press.

——— Rogers, A. G. & Tolman, D. L., eds. (1991), *Women, Girls & Psychotherapy: Reframing Resistance.* New York: Haworth Press.

Golding, W. (1954), *Lord of the Flies.* New York: Berkeley.

Goldner, V. (1991), Toward a critical relational theory of gender. *Psychoanal. Dial.*, 1:249–272.

Green, A. (2001), The intuition of the negative in playing and reality. In: *Squiggles and Spaces: Revisiting the Work of D. W. Winnicott, Vol. 1,* ed. M. Bertolini, A. Giannakoulas & M. Hernandez. London: Whurr, pp. 43–58.

Grosz, E. (1994), *Volatile Bodies: Toward a Corporeal Feminism.* Bloomington: Indiana University Press.

——— (1995), *Space, Time, and Perversion: Essays on the Politics of Bodies.* New York: Routledge.

Grotstein, J. S. (1993), Preface. In *Second Thoughts: Selected Papers on Psychoanalysis* by W. R. Bion. Northvale, NJ: Aronson, pp. xi–xxi.

Guntrip, H. (1971), *Psychoanalytic Theory, Therapy and the Self.* New York: Basic Books.

Gutwill, S. (1994a), Women's eating problems: Social context and the internalization of culture. In: *Eating Problems: A Feminist Psychoanalytic Treatment Model,* ed. C. Bloom, A. Gitter, S. Gutwill, L. Kogel & L. Zaphiropoulos. New York: Basic Books, pp. 1–27.

——— (1994b), The diet: Personal experience, social condition, and industrial empire. In: *Eating Problems: A Feminist Psychoanalytic Treatment Model,* ed. C. Bloom, A. Gitter, S. Gutwill, L. Kogel & L. Zaphiropoulos. New York: Basic Books, pp. 27–39.

Haaken, J. (1998), The recovery of memory, fantasy, and desire in women's trauma stories: Feminist approaches to sexual abuse and psychotherapy. In: *Women, Autobiography, Theory: A Reader,* ed. S. Smith & J. Watson. Madison: University of Wisconsin Press, pp. 352–366.

Hadley, M. (2003), Relational, indirect, adaptive, or just mean: Recent work on aggression in adolescent girls—part I. *Studies Gender & Sexual.,* 4:367–394.

——— (2004), Relational, indirect, adaptive, or just mean: Recent work on aggression in adolescent girls—part II. *Studies Gender & Sexual.,* 5:331–350.

Harris, A. (1997), Aggression, envy, and ambition: Circulating tensions in women's psychic life. *Gender & Psychoanal.,* 2:291–326.

——— (1998), The analyst as (auto)biographer. *Amer. Imago,* 55:255–275.

——— (2003), Misogyny: Hatred at close range. In: *Hating in the First Person Plural,* ed. D. Moss. New York: Other Press, pp. 249–278.

——— (2005), *Gender as Soft Assembly.* Hillsdale, NJ: The Analytic Press.

Harvey, E. D. (2002), Anatomies of rapture: Clitoral politics/medical blazons. *Signs,* 27:315–346.

Heberle, R. (1999), Disciplining gender: Or are women getting away with murder? *Signs,* 24:1103–1112.

Hegeman, E. (1995), Transferential issues in the psychoanalytic treatment of incest survivors. In: *Sexual Abuse Recalled: Treating Trauma in the Era of the Recovered Memory Debate,* ed. J. L. Alpert. Northvale, NJ: Aronson, pp. 185–214.

Heilbrun, C. G. (1988), *Writing a Woman's Life.* New York: Ballantine Books.

Henriques, J., Hollway, W., Urwin, C., Venn, C. & Walkerdine, V. (1984), *Changing the Subject: Psychology, Social Relations, and Subjectivity.* London: Methuen.

Hernandez, M. & Giannakoulas, A. (2001), On the construction of potential space. In: *Squiggles and Spaces: Revisiting the Work of D. W. Winnicott,*

Vol. 1, ed. M. Bertolini, A. Giannakoulas & M. Hernandez. London: Whurr, pp. 146–167.

Hesse-Biber, S. (1996), *Am I Thin Enough Yet? The Cult of Thinness and the Commercialization of Identity*. New York: Oxford University Press.

Hollway, W. (1989), *Subjectivity and Method in Psychology: Gender, Meaning and Science*. London: Sage.

Hopkins, B. H. (1997), Winnicott and the capacity to believe. *Internat. J. Psycho-Anal.*, 78:485–497.

Hoy, D. C. (2004), *Critical Resistance: From Poststructuralism to Post-Critique*. Cambridge, MA: MIT Press.

Josselson, R., ed. (1996), *Ethics and Process in the Narrative Study of Lives*. Thousand Oaks, CA: Sage.

Kelly, E. (1994), Pebble/shoe, CD by Eugenius, on *Mary Queen of Scots*, Atlantic Records.

Khan, M. M. (1993), Secret as potential space. In: *Between Reality and Fantasy: Winnicott's Concepts of Transitional Objects and Phenomena*, ed. S. A. Grolnick & L. Barkin. Northvale, NJ: Aronson, pp. 259–270.

Kierkegaard, S. (1980), *The Concept of Anxiety: A Simple Psychologically Orienting Deliberation on the Dogmatic Issue of Hereditary Sin*, ed. & trans. R. Thomte & A. B. Anderson. Princeton, NJ: Princeton University Press.

Knoblauch, S. (1997), The play and interplay of passionate experience: Multiple organizations of desire. *Gender & Psychoanal.*, 1:323–344.

——— (2000), *The musical Edge of Therapeutic Dialogue*. Hillsdale, NJ: The Analytic Press.

Kristeva, J. (1980), *Desire in language*. New York: Columbia University Press.

——— (1981), Women's time. In: *Feminism: An Anthology of Literary Theory and Criticism*, ed. R. R. Warhul & D. P. Herndl. New Brunswick, NJ: Rutgers University Press, pp. 860–879, 1997.

——— (1996), *Time and Sense: Proust and the Experience of Literature*, trans. R. Guberman. New York: Columbia University Press.

Kundera, M. (1984), *The Unbearable Lightness of Being*. New York: Harper & Row.

Lakoff, G. & Johnson, M. (1999), *Philosophy in the Flesh: The Embodied Mind and Its Challenge to Western Thought*. New York: Basic Books.

Lamb, S. (1999), *New Versions of Victims: Feminists Struggle with the Concept*. New York: New York University Press.

Lather, P. (1988), Feminist perspectives on empowering research methodologies. *Women's Stud. Internat. Forum*, 11:569–581.

——— & Smithies, C. (1997), *Troubling the Angels: Women Living with HIV/AIDS*. New York: Westview Press.

Layton, L. (1998), *Who's that girl? Who's that boy? Clinical Practice Meets Postmodern Gender Theory*. Hillsdale, NJ: The Analytic Press, 2004.
Lee, A. (1971), "A House Is Not a Motel," sound recording by Love, on *Forever Changes*, Elektra/Asylum.
Loewald, H. W. (1980), *Papers on Psychoanalysis*. New Haven, CT: Yale University Press.
Mahoney, M. A. & Yngvesson, B. (1992), The construction of subjectivity and the paradox of resistance: Reintegrating feminist anthropology and psychology. *Signs*, 18:44–73.
Manning, P. & Cullum-Swan, B. (1994), Narrative, content, and semiotic analysis. In: *Handbook of Qualitative Research*, ed. N. Denzin & Y. Lincoln. Newbury Park, CA: Sage, pp. 463–478.
Martin, E. (1987), *The Woman in the Body: A Cultural Analysis of Reproduction*. Boston, MA: Beacon Press.
McAdams, D. P. & Ochberg, R. L., eds. (1988), *Psychobiography and Life Narratives*. Durham, NC: Duke University Press.
McLane, J. (1996), The voice on the skin: Self-mutilation and Merleau-Ponty's theory of language. *Hypatia*, 11:107–118.
Merleau-Ponty, M. M. (1962), *The Phenomenology of Perception*, trans. C. Smith. London: Routledge & Kegan Paul, 1996.
Miller, N. K. (1991), *Getting Personal: Feminist Occasions and Other Autobiographical Acts*. London: Routledge.
Mitchell, S. A. (1993), *Hope and Dread in Psychoanalysis*. New York: Basic Books.
——— (1997), *Influence and Autonomy in Psychoanalysis*. Hillsdale, NJ: The Analytic Press.
——— (1998), From hosts to ancestors: The psychoanalytic vision of Hans Loewald. *Psychoanal. Dial.*, 8:825–856.
Mohanty, C. T. ((2004), *Feminism Without Borders: Decolonizing Theory, Practicing Solidarity*. Durham, NC: Duke University Press.
Mumby, D. K., ed. (1993), *Narrative and Social Control: Critical Perspectives*. Newbury Park, CA: Sage.
Naples, N., with Clark, E. (1996), Feminist participatory research and empowerment: Going public as survivors of childhood abuse. In: *Feminism and Social Change: Bridging Theory and Practice*, ed. H. Gottfried. Bloomington: Indiana University Press, pp. 160–183.
Nasser, M. (1997), *Culture and Weight Consciousness*. London: Routledge.
Ness, C. D. (2004), Why girls fight: Female youth violence in the inner city. *Annals Amer. Acad. Pol. & Soc. Sci.*, 595:32–48.
Novick, K. K. & Novick, J. (1987), The essence of masochism. *The Psychoanalytic Study of the Child*, 42:353–384. New Haven, CT: Yale University Press.

Ogden, T. (1989), *The Primitive Edge of Experience.* Northvale, NJ: Aronson.
——— (1992), The dialectically constituted/decentered subject of psychoanalysis III The contributions of Klein and Winnicott. *Internat. J. Psycho-Anal.*, 73:613–626.
——— (1994), *Subjects of Analysis.* Northvale, NJ: Aronson.
Orbach, S. (1986), *Hunger Strike: The Anorexic's Struggle as a Metaphor for Our Age.* New York: Norton.
Peterson, B. E. & Stewart, A. J. (1990), Using personal and fictional documents to assess psychosocial development: A case study of Vera Brittain's generativity. *Psychol. & Aging,* 5:400–411.
Pizer, S. A. (1998), *Building Bridges: The Negotiation of Paradox in Psychoanalysis.* Hillsdale, NJ: The Analytic Press.
Polkinghorne, D. (1991), Narrative and self-concept. *J. Narr. & Life Hist.*, 1:135–153.
——— (1996), Transformative narratives: From victimic to agentic life plots. *Amer. J. Occupat. There.*, 50:299–305.
Polivy, J. & Herman, C. P. (1985), Dieting and binging: A causal analysis. *Amer. Psycholog.*, 40:193–201.
Probyn, E. (1993), *Sexing the Self: Gendered Positions in Cultural Studies.* New York: Routledge.
Raghavan, C., Kavanagh, A., Gentile, K., Rajah, V. & Collado, L. (2005), Description of dating violence and associated community risk factors in an urban college sample. Presented at meeting of the American Psychology-Law Society Biennial Conference, March, La Jolla, CA.
Rajah, V., Raghavan, C. & Gentile, K. (2005), Gender differences in accounts for dating violence among a low income minority college sample. Presented at meeting of the American Psychology-Law Society Biennial Conference, March, La Jolla, CA.
Redfield, J. (1993), *The Celestine Prophesy: An Adventure.* New York: Warner Books.
Renik, O. (1995), The ideal of the anonymous analyst and the problem of self-disclosure. *Psychoanal. Quart.*, 64:466–495.
Rice, C. (1996), Trauma and eating problems: Expanding the debate. *Eating Disorders,* 4:197–237.
Richardson, L. (1995), Narrative and sociology. In: *Representation in Ethnography,* ed. J. Van Maanen. Thousand Oaks, CA: Sage, pp. 198–221.
Ricoeur, P. (1984), *Time and Narrative, Vol. 1,* trans. K. McLaughlin & D. Pellauer. Chicago: University of Chicago Press.
Riessman, C. K. (1993), *Narrative Analysis.* Newbury Park, CA: Sage.
Sampson, E. E. (1996), Establishing embodiment in psychology. *Theory & Psychol.*, 6:601–624.

Schwartz, M. F. & Gay, P. (1993), Physical and sexual abuse and neglect and eating disorder symptoms. *Eating Disorders*, 1:265–281.

Searles, H. F. (1979), *Countertransference and Related Subjects*. New York: International Universities Press.

Seid, R. P. (1994), Too "close to the bone": The historical context for women's obsession with slenderness. In: *Feminist Perspectives on Eating Disorders*, ed. P. Fallon, M. Katzman, & S. Wooley. New York: Guilford Press, pp. 3–16.

Sheldrake, R. (1990), *The Rebirth of Nature: The Greening of Science and God*. New York: Bantam Books.

Slavin, M. & Kriegman, D. (1998), Why the analyst needs to change: Toward a theory of conflict, negotiation, and mutual influence in the therapeutic process. *Psychoanal. Dial.*, 8:247–284.

Smith, S. (1993), *Subjectivity, Identity, and the Body: Women's Autobiographical Practices in the Twentieth Century*. Bloomington: Indiana University Press.

——— (1995), Performativity, autobiographical practice, resistance. *a/b: Auto/Biography Stud.*, 10:17–33.

——— & Watson, J., eds. (1998), *Women, Autobiography, Theory: A Reader*. Madison: University of Wisconsin Press.

Stacey, J. (1988), Can there be a feminist ethnography? *Women's Stud. Internat. Forum*, 11:21–27.

Stanley, L. (1993) The knowing because experiencing subject: Narratives, lives and autobiography. *Women's Stud. Internat. Forum*, 16:205–215.

——— (1996), The mother of invention: Necessity, writing and representation. *Feminism & Psychol.*, 6:45–51.

Suleiman, S. R., ed. (1985), *The Female Body in Western Culture: Contemporary Perspectives*. Cambridge, MA: Harvard University Press.

Sullivan, H. S. (1953), *The Interpersonal Theory of Psychiatry*. New York: Norton.

Synnott, A. (1991), *The Body Social: Symbolism, Self and Society*. New York: Routledge.

Thomas, J. (1996), *Time, Culture and Identity: An Interpretive Archaeology*. London: Routledge.

Tolman, D. L. & Brydon-Miller, M. (2001), *From Subjects to Subjectivities: A Handbook of Interpretive and Participatory Methods*. New York: New York University Press.

Trinh, T. (1989), *Women, Native, Other: Writing Postcoloniality and Feminism*. Bloomington: University of Indiana Press.

Turner, B. (1984), *The Body and Society*. Oxford: Basil Blackwell.

van der Kolk, B. A. (1994), The body keeps the score: Memory and the evolving psychobiology of posttraumatic stress. *Harvard Rev. Psychiat.*, 1:253–265.

Visweswaran, K. (1994), *Fictions of Feminist Ethnography*. Minneapolis: University of Minnesota Press.

von Sacher-Masoch, W. (1990), *The Confessions of Wanda von Sacher-Masoch*, trans. M. Phillips, C. Hébert & V. Vale. San Francisco: Re/Search.

Walkerdine, V. (1990), *Schoolgirl Fictions*. London: Verso.

——— (1994), Femininity as performance. In: *The Education Feminism Reader*, ed. L. Stone. New York: Routledge, pp. 57–72.

Warhol, R. R. & Herndl, D. P., eds. (1997), *Feminisms: An Anthology of Literary Theory and Criticism*. New Brunswick, NJ: Rutgers University Press.

Webster's II New College Dictionary (1999). New York: Houghton Mifflin.

Weitz, R., ed. (1998), *The Politics of Women's Bodies: Sexuality, Appearance, and Behavior*. New York: Oxford University Press.

West, B. A. (1992), Women's diaries as ethnographic resources. *J. Narr. & Life Hist.*, 2:333–354.

Widdershoven, G. & Smits, M. J. (1996), The story of life: Hermeneutic perspectives on the relationship between narrative and life history. *Narr. Stud. Lives*, 1:1–20.

Wiener, W. J. & Rosenwald, G. C. (1993), A moment's monument: The psychology of keeping a diary. *Narr. Stud. Lives*, 1:30–58.

Winnicott, D. W. (1958a), *Collected Papers: Through Paediatrics to Psycho-Analysis*. New York: Basic Books.

——— (1958b), The capacity to be alone. *Internat. J. Psycho-Anal.*, 39:416–420.

——— (1960), The theory of the parent-infant relationship. In: *Essential Papers in Object Relations*, ed. P. Buckley. New York: New York University Press, pp. 254–271, 1986.

——— (1970), On the basis for self in body. *Internat. J. Child Psychother.*, 1:7–16.

——— (1971), *Playing and Reality*. London: Tavistock/Routledge.

Winterson, J. (1985), *Oranges Are Not the Only Fruit*. New York: Grove Press.

Wolf, N. (1991), *The Beauty Myth: How Images of Beauty Are Used Against Women*. New York: Anchor Books.

Wooley, W. (1994), . . . And man created "woman": Representations of women's bodies in Western culture. In: *Feminist Perspectives on Eating Disorders*, eds. P. Fallon, M. Katzman & S. Wooley. New York: Guilford Press, pp. 17–52.

Young, K. (1991), Perspectives on embodiment: The uses of narrativity in ethnographic writing. *J. Narr. & Life Hist.*, 1:213–243.

Young-Bruehl, E. (1998), *Subject to Biography: Psychoanalysis, Feminism, and Writing Women's Lives*. Cambridge, MA: Harvard University Press.

Index